Denene Millner is articles editor at *Parenting* magazine. She is the author of *The Sistah's Rules*, and has coauthored, with her husband Nick Chiles, the novels *Love Don't Live Here Anymore* and *In Love and War*, and the nonfiction relationship series *What Brothers Think, What Sistahs Know*. She lives in South Orange, New Jersey, with her husband, two daughters, and stepson.

Angela Burt-Murray is the assistant managing editor at *Teen People* magazine. She has covered fashion, beauty, and health issues for *Honey*, *Essence*, *Teen People*, and *Black Elegance*. She also lives in South Orange, New Jersey, with her husband and two sons.

Mitzi Miller is an associate editor at *Jane* magazine, where she contributes to several departments, including "Eat." Formerly an associate entertainment editor at *Honey* magazine, where she popularized the adventurous "Road Trippin' " column, she now lives in New York City with her angry black dog, Drama.

THE ANGRY BLACK WOMAN'S GUIDE TO LIFE

Denene Millner
Angela Burt-Murray
Mitzi Miller

A PLUME BOOK

PLUME
Published by the Penguin Group
Penguin Group (USA) Inc., 375 Hudson Street, New York, New York 10014, U.S.A.
Penguin Books Ltd, 80 Strand, London WC2R 0RL, England
Penguin Books Australia Ltd, 250 Camberwell Road, Camberwell, Victoria 3124, Australia
Penguin Books Canada Ltd, 10 Alcorn Avenue, Toronto, Ontario, Canada M4V 3B2
Penguin Books India (P) Ltd, 11 Community Centre,
Panchsheel Park, New Delhi – 110 017, India
Penguin Books (N.Z.) Ltd, Cnr Rosedale and Airborne Roads,
Albany, Auckland 1310, New Zealand
Penguin Books (South Africa) (Pty) Ltd, 24 Sturdee Avenue,
Rosebank, Johannesburg 2196, South Africa

Penguin Books Ltd, Registered Offices: 80 Strand, London WC2R 0RL, England

First published by Plume, a member of Penguin Group (USA) Inc.

First Printing, April 2004
10 9 8 7 6 5 4 3 2 1

 REGISTERED TRADEMARK—MARCA REGISTRADA

LIBRARY OF CONGRESS CATALOGING-IN-PUBLICATION DATA
Millner, Denene.
The angry Black woman's guide to life / Denene Millner, Angela Burt-Murray, Mitzi Miller.
p. cm.
"A Plume book."
ISBN 0-452-28512-7 (trade pbk.)
1. African American women—Life skills guides.   2. African American women—Psychology.
I. Burt-Murray, Angela.   II. Miller, Mitzi.   III. Title.
E185.86.M545 2004
646.7'0089'96073—dc22   2003065623

Printed in the United States of America
Set in Galliard
Designed by Leonard Telesca

For ABWs everywhere, who love hard,
Dance with abandon, and Don't hesitate to
put 'em in their place.

Contents

ACKNOWLEDGMENTS

All praises due to the Almighty for His many blessings, even when I falter. Without him, surely, I'd be nothing. Thank you to my coauthor/baby daddy/husband/partner in crime Nick Chiles, for understanding the ways of this ABW, and loving me anyway; my beautiful princesses, Mari and Lila, for constantly making Mommy giggle (I thank God for you both, each and every day) and my shining star, Mazi; my parents, James and Bettye Millner, for raising their baby girl up proper, strong, and proud; my brother, Troy Millner, for giving me someone to look up to; and the entire Chiles family—Walter and Helen Chiles, Angelou, James, Miles and Cole Ezeilo, and Jamila Thornton and her lovely daughters Maia, Imani, and Zenzele—for loving me like I'm one of their own. Finally, thank you to my coauthors, Angela and Mitzi: You guys are the coolest, funniest, smartest, women I know. I'm so glad that God brought us together—thanks for being my friends. —With love, Denene

I dedicate this book to my favorite ABW: my grandmother Sadye M. Davis. Like most of us, this ABW's bark is way worse than her bite. And to my mother, Diana, and my father, Howard, thank you for always believing in me and for knowing before I even knew that this was possible. To my brother Bryan for his gentle wisdom. Big thanks to my sister-in-law Tracey for baby-sitting when I was supposed to be writing! And a big kiss-covered thanks to my husband, Leonard Murray, for his unwavering support, inspiration for Chapter 7, and for blessing me every day with something from Chapter 13—we'll talk about number 77 soon. To the sunshine in my life, Solomon and Ellison, with whom Mommy can never stay angry. To my three-times-dope partners Denene and Mitzi, thank you for the blood, sweat, tears, and jokes. May we always have each other's backs! You know a sistah got gifts! —With love, Angela

I would like to dedicate this book to God, Yemaya, and all the orishas that guide and protect me along my path. To my mother and best friend in the entire universe, Elsa Miller—you are my ABW idol; Melissa Miller, because being my little sister is one of the hardest jobs in the world; my Tia, when all else fails you are always there; and my father, Guillermo Miller: You are the meter by which all men are measured. I'd also like to thank all of my family and friends for believing, supporting, and encouraging me through this confusion called my life; A. Barnett, for opening the first door; K. Borders for the late-night support; and, finally, my coauthors/partners in the come-up, Denene and Angela—thank you for being my Michelle and Kelly. —With love, Mitzi

The ABWs would also like to acknowledge our capable

agent, Victoria Sanders, a true AWW in her own right, our editor, Laurie Chittenden, for just, like, getting us, and her faithful sidekick, Erika Kahn, for guiding this train into the station (you may not have gotten it when you wanted it, but you got it on time!).

THE ANGRY BLACK WOMAN'S GUIDE TO LIFE

1

i'M an ABW anD PROUD OF iT!*

There we were, trying our best to come up with something funny, interesting, and provocative to put into the humor section of our magazine, when Angela sent an e-mail proposing a hilarious story on a fake service she'd conjured up at her computer: "What if," she wrote, "we created an Internet service called angryblackwoman.com, where people can sign up to have someone that did them wrong cursed out good and righteous, for a low fee of $19.95 a month— 'cause, you know don't nobody curse somebody out like a sistah (unlimited recipients, of course). People would answer a questionnaire to complete their 'custom curse-out,' and we could all come up with a list of people most likely to need this service."

Laughter could be heard from all corners of the office

(even the lone white woman on the magazine staff laughed and offered up someone to curse out)—and, suddenly, the e-mails were flying: "I'd send someone to curse out the man who consistently misses child support payments," one said. "I'd send a cuss out to the guy who always promises to call but never, ever, ever does," another said. "The one manager who keeps calling me in to do 'one last thing' when she sees me with my coat on—knowing the hair salon closes in a hour and it's all the way uptown? She has one coming!" another shouted out loud.

We all fell out in laughter—and within minutes, our corner of the office was abuzz. Want us to bring snotty-nosed children that will call the intended recipient daddy on cue? No problem. Need her to wear a magenta mini-dress and fling herself over the coffin of a no-good somebody? Bet. Cursing out white folks? That'll definitely cost extra, because you don't just curse out white folks and get away with it (they're quick to dial 911). Oh, the options were endless.

And then the conversation turned serious: Why was it so easy for black women to not only identify with angryblackwomen.com, but want to sign up for the service and be a part of it?

Because we could all relate.

When most people think about angry black women (ABW), they think of it in a negative, stereotypical, neck-swizzling, eye-rolling, and, worst of all, dismissive kind of way—as if whenever we have an opinion, or stand up for ourselves, that we have an attitude problem, that we're miserable, that we need a man. That we're just plain mad. But you know what? We're not mad. We don't have attitude problems. We're not miserable. We're angry for a reason. We black women have to work three times as hard to get half the respect and significantly less pay to simply be in the room with everyone else—and the thanks we get for it is people trying to dismiss us: "Oh, don't mind her, she's just an *angry black woman*."

And while employers, spouses, and strangers try to dismiss us with these three simple words, there's one thing anyone with even half a brain and a cursory knowledge of black women fear from an ABW: the blackout. This apocalyptic event—that usually begins with a rapid-fire litany of choice words (most of which are of the four-letter persuasion and therefore unprintable in this book) and ends with the transgressor in the fetal position calling for his or her mother—is unleashed when an ABW loses her natural mind and cuts loose on someone who has committed an unforgivable slight, injustice, or insult. And while many try to lampoon these apocalyptic events as stereotypical neck-wiggling behavior, sometimes a good, old-fashioned tongue-lashing is just what some people need to give us our propers, as Aretha would say.

Look, the truth of the matter is that every black woman—

whether she is from the projects or a member of the Opal Circle, whether she is on welfare or bringing in a six-figure paycheck—knows that we are a strong, proud people who are opinionated and confident enough with ourselves to voice it. Throughout history, angry black women have moved mountains. It wasn't until Rosa Parks got angry about the lynching of Emmett Till that she decided not to move from her bus seat—an angry black woman's strike that ushered in the civil rights movement. Aretha Franklin wasn't exactly cooing when she demanded her man give her R-E-S-P-E-C-T— and her fans who could relate, black women, put her at the top of the charts because they *felt* her. Anita Hill had to be damn angry to suffer the abuse of Congress to point the sexual harassment finger at Clarence Thomas; she may not have won the battle, but she sure as shooting let black folks know that Thomas was no Thurgood Marshall. We've had our eye on him ever since. Simply put, sometimes anger spurs progress.

So we decided to claim it, embrace it, and make it ours: We're angry black women and damn proud. Here, our tribute to angry black women everywhere. Part social commentary, part riff, this tongue-in-cheek read explores the history of the angry black woman, the different types of angry black women, the manifestation of angry black women in entertainment and media, and the reason why we're so mad, along with the top words, actions, and deeds that everyone from an employer to a child can do to tick off an angry black woman. *The Angry Black Woman's Guide to Life* will also help others—men, employers, children, random people in the street—come to this understanding: An angry black woman is not to be messed with.

2

WHaT TYPe oF ABW ARe YoU?

Many people try to label us like we're all the same—but we're not. When it comes to correcting those that dare to step to us with nonsense, we all deal with our anger in different ways. Take our quiz to find out what type of ABW you are.

The Quiz

1. As you're getting ready for an evening out with your girlfriends, your man comments that your dress is fitting a little snug around the hips. You reply:

   A. "Maybe if I hadn't spent 36.5 hours in labor pushing out your bad-ass kids, I could fit into my dress and catch a new man."

B. You agree with him and buy an expensive new designer dress the next day with *his* credit card.

C. You agree with him, cancel your plans, and sign up for a gym membership in the morning.

2. After an exhausting day of work, grocery shopping, preparing dinner, and tidying up around the apartment, your husband nudges you just as you start to fall asleep and asks for a little sumthin' sumthin'. Do you:

A. Say, "Sure, but then how am I going to get back to sleep after these two minutes of pleasure?"

B. Say, "Sure." And go into the bathroom with your vibrator.

C. Say, "Love to, sweetie. After all, I don't need more than three hours of sleep anyway."

3. After forgetting your birthday, you confront your man and:

A. Show up at his job and start singing, "Happy Birthday to Me" in front of all his coworkers.

B. Tell him it's okay and make a mental note to plan a vacation with the girls during his birthday weekend.

C. Say, "It's no big deal. The only present I want is to be with you."

4. When the company newsletter announces the latest round of promotions, you see that Perky Paula, your underqualified assistant with the 36Ds, has been promoted over you. You:

   A. Take the stack of undelivered newsletters and start a bonfire in front of your boss's office.
   B. Xerox the hotel receipts from your manager's expense report from the "long lunches" with Paula and mail them anonymously to his wife and his boss.
   C. Congratulate Paula and sign up for another continuing education course.

5. The office suck-up tells your boss that she saw you at a party on the night you asked to leave early for a family emergency. You:

   A. Corner her in the ladies' room and loudly tell her, "You besta keep my name out of your mouth."
   B. Change her voice-mail greeting to say, "She's no longer with the firm as she has been hospitalized for a stress-related illness."
   C. Apologize profusely to your boss and work late for the next month to earn back her trust.

6. One of your coworkers always forwards sexist e-mails around the office. After he sends one with a character that physically resembles you, you:

A. Tell him to call building security because they are the only ones that will be able to pull the "black ass" he's so fond of talking about off of him.
B. Break into his e-mail after hours and forward all his dirty e-mails to human resources.
C. Send back an e-mail that says: "You so crazy."

7. When you realize you're being stalked by store security at your favorite boutique for "Shopping While Black," you:

A. Whip out your cell phone and tell the rent-a-cop that you're Johnnie Cochran's niece and you'd be more than happy to get your uncle on the phone for him to explain why he's all up in your business.
B. You immediately leave humiliated and wage a campaign to boycott the store.
C. Buy the most expensive thing in the store to prove that you're a good Negro and can afford to be there.

8. While at a restaurant, the diners next to your table make a racist comment about their waitress, another African American woman. You:

A. Turn to your dining companion and loudly tell your own racist joke so that they can hear.

B. Hip the waitress to the joke and suggest she serve a "special" helping of the restaurant's secret sauce.

C. Ignore them.

9. While sitting in class you overhear two white students saying that the only reason you're in law school is because of affirmative action. You:

   A. Tell them that being a legacy was the only reason their "low-LSAT-scoring-donation-giving-foundation-starting-daddy-called-in-a-favor" dumb asses were able to get in anyway.

   B. Have your hookup in the admission's office Xerox their sub-par transcripts and post them all over campus.

   C. Engage them in a friendly debate about affirmative action.

10. During the new Morris Chestnut movie you've been dying to see, the mostly black audience continuously erupts in loud chatter, cell phone conversations, babies crying, couples making out noisily. You:

   A. Keep your mouth shut because you know the theater is full of other angry black women. You'll buy a bootleg video of the movie next week.

   B. Tell the manager on your way out to see the same movie in the white neighborhood.

C. Get beat down after you shush folks one too many times.

11. Your chronically overbooked hairstylist catches an attitude with you when you ask her to hurry up with your hair because you're going to be late for a concert. You:

   A. Snatch the hot comb out of her hand and threaten to straighten her out if she doesn't fix your do quick, fast, and fly.

   B. Hair undone, you leave and on your way out book your next appointment with her rival stylist.

   C. Call a friend and offer her your tickets.

12. A guard at airport security singles you out of the line of passengers to go through your carry-on and makes comments to her girlfriend on your lingerie as she pulls it out of your bag. You:

   A. Thank her for her attention to detail and tell her how sorry you are that her career goal is to check stranger's underwear.

   B. After clearing the checkpoint you go to the manager's office and tell her supervisor that she failed to check some compartments in your bag.

   C. Wait patiently and offer to open things she hasn't even asked about.

13. Your child's school calls you at work to notify you of your son's suspension for starting a food fight in the cafeteria. You:

   A. Storm out of the office and surprise your juvenile delinquent as school lets out with a beating of a lifetime.
   B. Go home and remove all entertainment-related material from his room and change the family answering machine message to say: "Michael will no longer be allowed to use the phone until he learns to put food in his mouth, not in the air."
   C. Retain an attorney to defend your sweet angel against these "slanderous accusations."

14. You come home early from work and catch your daughter and her boyfriend on the sofa in a compromising position. You:

   A. Chase them both around the block half naked.
   B. Sneak upstairs and call his mother to come over and witness her son's imminent demise.
   C. Pass out from the shame.

15. Your three-year-old toddler goes with you to the grocery store and, upon entering the candy aisle, proceeds to fall out because you refuse his repeated request for

supersugary treats, causing everyone in a three-aisle vicinity to gawk and stare. You:

A. Snatch him up by the arm, as his feet dangle a foot from the floor, and hiss at all those who dare watch to mind their own damn business, or they're next.
B. Load the cart up with all his favorite treats to quiet him down, then leave them at the checkout counter.
C. Abandon your cart, leave, and go shopping another day when junior's in a better mood.

16. As you're finalizing the details for your child's birthday party, you open your child's report card and see that the budding rocket scientist has managed to go from A's and B's to C's and D's. You:

A. Xerox a copy of the report card and send it to all those invited, noting that this is why the party was canceled.
B. Let your child think the party is still on, and then when he arrives, the only guest is a tutor.
C. Continue with your plans for the party because now is when he really needs the support of his friends.

The Answer Key

For each "A," give yourself 8 points.
For each "B," give yourself 4 points.
For each "C," give yourself 1 point.

If you scored above 89, you are the Curse-You-Out-in-a-Heartbeat Angry Black Woman. Let's get ready to rumble! This ABW is no joke. Sistah girl is like a world-class boxer who will pummel those who would dare spar with her. Always on high alert of any little slight, real or imagined, this ABW has been known to knock out opponents with a blistering combination of body blows (comments about victims' physical appearance) and the crowd favorite, the below-the-belt blow (remarks about home life or sexual prowess). Most opponents don't last the second round and are often left in tears, catatonic states of shock, mouths agape in front of sell-out crowds.

Famous ABWs: Aunt Esther from *Sanford and Son,* Mary J. Blige, Mo'Nique

If you scored 65 to 89 points, you are the Silent-Stewer-That-Plots-Your-Demise Angry Black Woman. The most deadly of the three ABWs, she's like a secret agent. Her skills are often underestimated by opponents who think they've gotten away with humiliating or dissing her. While she often lets minor incidents slide, major offenses cause her to reach into her arsenal. With a keen eye for details and maximum damage, opponents are dealt with in a stealth-like manner. The sneak attack is her weapon of choice—just when her opponents think she's forgotten about an unfortunate incident, she strikes. Victims are often left homeless, with their credit in shreds, wardrobes aflame, or crying uncontrollably on talk shows.

Famous ABWs: Bernadine from *Waiting to Exhale,* Diana Ross

If you scored under 65 points, you are the In-Denial Angry Black Woman. This ABW has a difficult time tapping into her anger. It's so deeply buried that she always appears to put on a cheery face and accepts whatever life dishes out. She has difficulty believing that anyone would intentionally do her wrong and tends to shoulder the blame for family drama or work problems. In conversation she's always heralded as the "superwoman" and inevitably winds up in a rubber room. Her only victim is her personal sanity.

Famous ABWs: Claire Huxtable, Condoleezza Rice

3

A HiSTORY LeSSon: ABWS Who Have Changed The WORLD

Angry black women have contributed much to society: When black women get sick and tired of being sick and tired, revolutionary change occurs. Witness the legacy of the patron saint of historical ABWs, Sojourner Truth. Born into slavery as Isabella Van Wagener in 1797, she escaped with her youngest child into freedom just before emancipation and, with the support of the bold new black rights laws, successfully sued an Alabama plantation for the freedom of one of her sons. Later, she worked as a street preacher who became one of the most vociferous voices in the women's movement, using her experiences as a slave and a fiery tongue to lead the charge for equality. Truth's 1851 speech before the Women's Rights Convention in Akron, Ohio, is one of legend: In it, she railed against an agenda that was focused solely on suffrage for white women, delivering a tongue-lashing ABWs envy to this very day. Abolitionist and convention president Frances D. Gage later recounted the speech that would become the classic expression of women's rights:

> *That man over there says that women need to be helped into carriages and lifted over ditches, and to have the best place everywhere. Nobody ever helps* me *into carriages, or over mud puddles, or gives me any best place. And ain't I a woman? Look at me! Look at my arm* [she bared her right arm and flexed her powerful muscles]. *I have plowed and planted and gathered into barns, and no man could head me. And ain't I a woman? I could work as much and eat as much as man—when I could get it—and bear the lash as well! And ain't I a woman? I have borne children and seen most of them sold into slavery, and when I cried out with a mother's grief, none but Jesus heard me. And ain't I a woman? . . . That little man in back there! He says women can't have as much rights as men. 'Cause Christ wasn't a woman. Where did your Christ come from? Where did your Christ come from? From God and a Woman! Man had nothing to do with him! If the first woman God ever made was strong enough to turn the world upside down all alone, these women together ought to be able to turn it back and get it right side up*

again. And now that they are asking to do it, the men better let them.

By the time Sojourner finished, everyone was standing on their feet—the room exploding in thunderous applause.

ABWs, you have a proud history. It is this same fiery spirit that has coursed through the veins of women that freed slaves, galvanized the civil rights movement, and even helped send Mae C. Jemison, the first African American woman, into space.

THROUGH THE YEARS

Harriet Tubman, conductor on the Underground Railroad (1820–1913)

Why she was angry: She was a slave that had her children sold away from her.

What her anger accomplished: After escaping from slavery herself, the woman called Moses is credited with risking her life to free more than 300 people from slavery.

Sojourner Truth, preacher and women's rights activist (1797–1883)

Why she was angry: Because white women wouldn't accept the fact that we were in the struggle together.

What her anger accomplished: Opened the ranks of the women's rights movement to include black women's issues.

Josephine Baker, dancer and singer (1906–1975)
Why she was angry: Because of America's racist laws and attitudes, she was forced to leave the country to pursue her passion for entertaining.
What her anger accomplished: This well-respected, groundbreaking performer, who, despite being one of the most sought-after performers of her time, was often the victim of racial segregation, took a stand and left America for Europe. In her quest to show that we are all human—and that color should have very little to do with the way we treat each other—she adopted and raised more than a dozen children of all races and ethnicities. She also helped introduce Europe to black artistic culture.

Angela Davis, political activist (1944–)
Why she was angry: Despite the strides made during the civil rights movement, race relations were still at a standstill.
What her anger accomplished: Davis was an integral part of the Black Panther movement, spread the civil rights message, and sparked a revolution.

Rosa Parks, civil rights icon (1913–)

Why she was angry: After learning of the death of Emmett Till, the seamstress refused to yield her seat on the bus.

What her anger accomplished: Her detainment by the police galvanized the civil rights movement.

Ida B. Wells, journalist and antilynching activist (1862–1931)

Why she was angry: The lynching of black men and women throughout the South, including three close friends

What her anger accomplished: She is credited with sounding a national alarm about this crime by writing articles, lecturing, and founding antilynching societies.

Anita Hill, professor (1956–)

Why she was angry: A former employer she accused of sexually harassing her was nominated to the U.S. Supreme Court.

What her anger accomplished: Her televised testimony ushered in the sexual harassment awareness movement and the passing of legislation to protect women in the workplace.

Shirley Chisholm (1924–)

Why she was angry: Having worked as an expert in early childhood education and the New York City Bureau of

Child Welfare, she knew up close and personal what the lack of government help meant for the urban poor: They just got more poor.

What her anger accomplished: She decided to change the system from within. In 1968, she was elected to the U.S. House of Representatives as a Democrat—the first black woman to ever serve in that body. She quickly gained national attention as an outspoken critic of the Vietnam War and the plight of the urban poor. Without her, the government would have continued to ignore us and our problems, which were ultimately America's problems.

Marian Anderson, singer (1897–1993)

Why she was angry: In 1939, after being invited to sing at Constitution Hall in Washington, D.C., she was denied access by the Daughters of the American Revolution (DAR).

What her anger accomplished: Undaunted by their banishment, Anderson sang on the steps of the Lincoln Memorial in front of 75,000 people on Easter morning, at the invitation of First Lady Eleanor Roosevelt, who publicly resigned from the DAR, thereby calling national attention to black Americans' struggle for equality.

Winnie Mandela, political activist (1936–)

Why she was angry: The subjugation of her fellow South

Africans and the twenty-five–year imprisonment of her husband, Nelson Mandela

What her anger accomplished: She rallied the country and the international community against apartheid and helped to bring down the racist Afrikaner government.

4

Take This Job and Shove It: ABWs at Work

Everybody's got to work to survive—but surviving work is a different story, especially for an ABW. There's never enough time, enough pay, or, more importantly, enough respect for what an ABW contributes to her workplace. Sure, sure—recent studies show that now, more than ever, black women are making great strides in the workplace, assuming more management roles, making more money. Indeed, *Newsweek* magazine recently filled its pages with black women claiming that it's never been a better time to be a black woman at work.

But let's be clear: Zora Neale Hurston once wrote that black women "are da mules of the world," and her words ring just as true today. We're constantly expected to take this job and love it—all the while having our motives and moves second-guessed. Our intense focus is often mistaken for a bad attitude; initiative translates to aggressiveness. If we take on additional responsibility, we're labeled domineering. And expressing an opinion contrary to our peers? Well, that's reduced to combativeness.

Between backstabbing coworkers and ineffective managers, an eight-hour workday can seem like endless torture. So what's an ABW to do?

For starters, take a page from our illustrious patron saint Florence, the sharp-tongued, quick-witted "household technician" on the TV classic *The Jeffersons*. Each episode, our heroine traded barbs with her Napoleonic, loudmouthed boss, George Jefferson, whose greatest pleasure in life is administering a lengthy list of mind-numbing chores. Of course, while George was consumed with micromanaging her workday and demanding that she answer the door, he clearly overlooked that not only did Florence fulfill all of her mandated duties as a housekeeper—their Park Avenue apartment was immaculate—she kept the household running like clockwork, raised the snot-nosed son, Lionel, and held wife Weezie's hand through all of George's drama. All of this is to say that like the true ABW that she was, Florence always got the job done—plus some—despite little reward, recognition, or respect.

The beauty of Florence, though, was that she never took any mess. Each time George lobbed yet another ridiculous request her way, she stood firm, stuck up for herself, and put everybody in their respective place—without losing her gig. You, too, can do it. Here we present some guidelines for ABWs looking to get through the work experience with their sanity intact and their paycheck direct-deposited in their bank accounts.

Politically Correct Ways for ABWs to Survive Corporate America

The workplace can be a minefield of potentially career-destroying situations. How an ABW deals with them determines whether she climbs the corporate ladder or ends up on the unemployment line. ABWs are survivors. Here are the do's and don'ts to learn how to master the game.

How to Deal with the Backstabbing Coworker

Scenario: Once again, while in an important meeting with senior management, your office nemesis presents the cost-saving idea you've been working on for the past six months as her own.

Don't: Leap across the conference table in a single bound and beat her in the head with the company ethics policy handbook.

Do: Speak up for yourself. In a nonconfrontational way, thank your coworker for opening the floor to your idea, whip out your professionally prepared graphics and spreadsheets to illustrate your concept, and walk management through your idea. After the meeting, schedule an appointment with your supervisor to discuss your coworker's behavior.

How to Deal with a Bad Manager

Scenario: Your boss, who's notoriously bad with deadlines, keeps making you work late to help her get back on track and not look like the incompetent manager that she is.

Don't: Don't announce to everyone that this is the last time she's going to mess up your weekly hair appointment, then grab your purse, run to the ladies' room, and escape through the air shaft to freedom.

Do: Schedule a morning meeting with her to discuss deadlines and explain to her that while you're a team player and would love to stay and help, you have prior commitments. Ask her what you can do during the workday to assist everyone in meeting deadlines.

How to Deal with Tasks Outside Your Job Description

Scenario: Your boss interrupts you while you're completing a time-sensitive project to request that you run and pick up an anniversary present for his wife and roses for his girlfriend.

Don't: Look at him like he's got five heads and tell him, "Sure, I'll get right on it as soon as you show me in my job description where it says I'm supposed to run your personal errands."

Do: Send him an e-mail explaining how his request made you uncomfortable, but that you took the liberty of looking up the phone numbers for the florist and a personal shopper at Saks Fifth Avenue to help him out "this time." Print out a copy of this e-mail and keep it for your records.

How to Change Jobs

Scenario: After being passed over yet again for a promotion, and having yet another request for a raise turned down, you've decided it's time to find a new gig.

Don't: Send a long e-mail to your supervisor—and CC everyone in your department—listing all your grievances and her management shortcomings, then flip everyone the bird as you stomp out the door.

Do: Find another job, submit your two-week notice, and use your exit interview with human resources to explain what the company is losing with your departure.

How to Deal with Sexual Harassment

Scenario: Your department head calls you into the office and, while you're discussing your latest project, invites you along for a getaway weekend in the Caribbean to discuss your upcoming promotion and raise.

Don't: Fling the door open and curse him out from top to bottom so that the entire office can hear about his indecent proposal.

Do: Politely decline the offer, excuse yourself from the office, and head directly to human resources.

The Best and Worst Jobs for ABWs

Positions of authority are a must, as ABWs were born to tell people what to do, not be ordered around. We've compiled a list of the best and worst jobs for ABWs.

Best Job	Why	Worst Job	Why
Police officer	Not only do you get to maintain order and carry a gun and handcuffs, as a special bonus you can use the siren to get you to your hair appointment on time.	Security guard	You just can't get people to listen to you if all you have is a whistle and a flashlight.
Principal	With authority over the students, teachers, and administrative staff, you're the queen of all you survey.	Teacher	Since most schools have outlawed corporal punishment, you have to rule with fear and intimidation, and that doesn't always work with today's ADD-rattled children.
Airline pilot	Nobody's allowed in the cockpit, and when you go on the loudspeaker and say, "This is your captain speaking," everyone shuts the hell up and listens.	Taxi driver	Road Rage is your middle name. Nuff said.
Store manager	You get to make your own schedule, use a hefty store discount, get the first look at all the new merchandise, and the power to hire all your friends.	Salesclerk	Come on, you'll be dealing with whiny customers trying to squeeze their big butts into the merchandise all day long. And you can't ever cuss them out or tell them they look crazy because the customer is always right.

Best Job	Why	Worst Job	Why
Human resource VP	With access to everyone's personal information and salaries, you get to know all the dirt and use it accordingly.	Administrative assistant	With responsibilities that include getting coffee, answering phones, and lying to his wife about his whereabouts, this is just a fancy title for flunky.
Judge	This is the ultimate position for an ABW. Not only do you get to tell people how jacked up they are, but you also get to level punishment for the unfortunate souls forced to go before you.	Bailiff	You have to stand all day, wear a polyester uniform, and you only get to crack heads if someone acts up.

5

WELL-MEANING RACISTS: SOMETIMES THEY SAY THE STUPIDEST THINGS

Admit it: There's been at least one time in your life that some person, under the guise of innocent curiosity, has asked you something so perfectly ridiculous that you had to pause and look around in search of the hidden camera and ask yourself, "He's kidding, right?" Their questions could be about anything—personal hygiene, race relations, marital status. And they all have one thing in common: They're totally inappropriate and completely insensitive.

Don't get us wrong, we're not against someone asking us questions. It's just that these seemingly innocent queries are almost always based on hurtful stereotypes and often require us to bear the burden of speaking for the entire black race. News flash: We're neither ghetto tour guides nor national spokeswomen for black girls everywhere.

Of course, our natural inclination is to put anyone who steps to us with such silly questions in their place, with a few expletives thrown in for good measure. But blacking out on these people will get you absolutely nowhere (except maybe jail, as they are prone to call the cops on an ABW when they feel threatened). So instead we suggest you take a page from our patron saint Star Jones, celebrity lawyer and talk-show host on the hugely popular ABC show *The View*. The beauty of Star is that she speaks her mind, with attitude, intelligence, and grace, the three things any ABW worth her salt must carry in her verbal arsenal to combat misguided people. One gets the sense that Star has earned her stripes to get where she is today—she's a plus-sized woman in an industry that puts more stock in your dress size than in your true ability. But she manages to stand up for herself and other black women without being caustic and falling into the "bitter black woman" trap.

To help you do the same, we've created some of the scenarios that we—and you, undoubtedly—have encountered. You know the questions: they range from "Do you wash your hair every day?" to "You don't experience racism, do you?" But instead of reaching out and touching them really hard, or silently stewing over the response you wish you would have said, we've created some scenarios and responses that will allow you to put them in their place, move race relations forward, and leave with your head held high.

1. **What they say:** "I have a lot of black friends."

    What they're thinking: Let me clearly establish that I'm not a racist before she starts in on that slavery psychobabble they're always heaving on us.

    What an ABW wants to say: Whoop-de-doo. Do you want a medal for this? Do you collect black friends like a stamp collector? Has having black friends become an Olympic sport or is this your way of trying to say you're down. Do you think your "black friends" like you or maybe they just want to be able to say they have a lot of white friends, too? I'm quite sure at this very moment they are somewhere laughing at you because when you met them you said: "I have a lot of black friends."

    What an ABW should say: Depending on the environment (work, party, random stranger in line at the bank), you should temper your response as to avoid termination, expulsion from social settings, or arrest. Pat the person on the shoulder and say, "Good for you. Black people love it when white people accept them into their circle. I'm sure they're better people for knowing a culturally sensitive person such as yourself."

2. **What they say:** "Can I touch your hair?"

    What they're thinking: Eww, I heard you people wash your hair only once a month. I wonder what that feels like.

    What an ABW wants to say: Hell no, you can't touch

my hair. I neither know where your nasty fingers have been nor do I know you like that. Put your hands on me and I will smack the taste out of your mouth.

What an ABW should say: Well, Jack, I consider my body to be my temple and my hair to be my crown, and I don't really like people to put their hands on my head. It's an extremely personal act. But thank you for taking so much interest in my personal grooming.

3. **What they say:** "You (or some other professional black person) are so articulate."

What they're thinking: Damn. She actually knows how to conjugate verbs. I didn't know they taught that at those run-down public schools they go to.

What an ABW wants to say: I would think so after four years of college, a master's degree, and a few continuing education courses on the side, but you probably wouldn't know that since this is the first time you're speaking to me and not just ordering me to do something. And I wish I could say the same for your ignorant ass, but since you constantly send out memos riddled with grammatical errors, clearly I can't. Exactly how you managed to become vice president baffles me.

What an ABW should say: Why thank you for commenting on my diction. As a well-educated and accomplished professional, I and my family pride ourselves on always being well-spoken. But I have to be honest with

you. Sometimes it is difficult when I run into less edu-
cated people and I find myself having to use words with
fewer syllables in order to make myself understood. It's so
laborious . . . I mean hard.

4. **What they say:** "You're so exotic-looking. Where are you
from?"
What they're thinking: She's so much prettier than
the black women I'm used to seeing. She can't be from
around here. She's probably easy. They all are.
What an ABW wants to say: Where the hell do you
think I'm from, dummy? I live around the corner from
you and your wife. And no, you cannot sleep with me.
Get the hell out of my face before I call my cousin Roy
and dem to whoop your butt for disrespecting me.
What an ABW should say: Why thank you so much
for the compliment. I appreciate your going out of
your way to flatter me, but, quite honestly, I don't think
I'm any more "exotic" than the last black woman that
walked by.

5. **What they say:** "How many kids do you have?"
What they're thinking: I wonder how many of her kids
I'm supporting with my tax dollars.
What an ABW wants to say: Why do you assume that I
have children? Contrary to what Hollywood, the govern-
ment, nightly news, and rap videos suggest, not all black

women are breeding like fruit flies. My mother, who was married to my father, raised me right. And I don't know nothin' about birthing no babies.

What an ABW should say: You're so perceptive. I'm so flattered that after just meeting me you've assessed that I'm such a kind and nurturing woman that I would make an outstanding mother to any number of children. While I haven't had the pleasure of giving birth, I look forward to it.

6. **What they say:** "Are the projects as bad as they look on TV?"

   What they're thinking: All black people come from the hood.

   What an ABW wants to say: Why don't we pack up all your little things and drop you off down there this evening? That way you can get the up close and personal view of project life. I'm sure some of the local folks would love to answer all your questions. I, on the other hand, won't be able to be your ghetto tour guide because I grew up in the town your parents couldn't afford to live in.

   What an ABW should say: Honestly, I don't like to pass judgment on things I don't have any personal knowledge of. But my education has taught me that most things you see on television tend to be overexaggerated.

7. **What they say:** You were a part of that affirmative action program, right?

   What they're thinking: Clearly, you're not qualified to be here, and if it wasn't for that government handout, you'd never be in my office.

   What an ABW wants to say: Well, perhaps if my father was frat buddies with the president of the company and able to make a call to good ol' Uncle Jimmy to get me your position, I wouldn't have had to work twice as hard, logged three times as many hours working, and still have to answer to you, then there would never be a question as to the effectiveness of the affirmative action program that turned me down because I was overqualified.

   What an ABW should say: Actually, I'm not a part of that program, but it's good to know you're such a strong supporter of such an important resource for diversity at this company.

8. **What they say:** What's wrong with those gangsta rappers?

   What they're thinking: I know you know all of them personally. You probably know all the lyrics, have been in a few videos, and identify with the "struggle."

   What an ABW wants to say: Considering the fact that the vast amount of rap music is purchased by young white teens, perhaps you might want to consult with your son after he emerges from his room, where, after putting on his Sean John velour sweatsuit, he was probably busy making pipe bombs and plotting to stuff his girlfriend in a trunk and drive her off a bridge because Eminem said to.

What an ABW should say: Honestly, as a cultural expression, hip-hop has always been a means for people to express oppression, injustice, and the will it takes to live under such dire circumstances. So while I'm no gangsta rap aficionada, I would imagine that many of these artists are just expressing themselves and their community's frustrations—much like John Lennon.

9. **What they say:** "I don't see color; I wouldn't care if you were green."

What they're thinking: I don't care about your skin color until you try to marry my son and move in next door.

What an ABW wants to say: The very fact that you're commenting on my color tells me that you're extremely conscious of my color, and if I were green, you should care, because clearly I would not be from this planet.

What an ABW should say: Correct me if I'm wrong, but I think what you're trying to say is that you don't judge people by the color of their skin. It's okay to notice that people are different. In fact, I would want you to recognize me as a black woman because I'm very proud of who I am.

10. **What they say:** "Why are you so angry?"

   What they're thinking: Slavery is over, and I didn't have anything to do with it anyway. Why can't they just get over it and move on?

   What an ABW wants to say: Read this book.

   What an ABW should say: Read this book.

6

OTHER BLACK FOLK: SOMETIMES WE'RE OUR OWN WORST ENEMY

Black folks' most embarrassing moments usually start with a live press conference. The Politician steps to the podium in a ballroom in an expensive downtown hotel. The room is packed with a rabid crowd of cameramen, photographers, newscasters, newspaper journalists, and, of course, the tabloid reporters who originally broke the scandalous story. The Politician's once dignified and camera-ready features are solemn. The newspaper journalists whisper to themselves that he appears aged in the last forty-eight hours. The proud shoulders that once held the weight of black America's ills on it are slumped. The custom European suit, which put him on *People* magazine's best-dressed politicos list two years in a row, hangs on his thinning frame.

Never one to face the music alone, the Politician is flanked by his trusted personal minister/spiritual adviser and his wife.

Always perfectly coiffed, even in times of tragedy, the Wife (not a strand of her Diahann Carroll roasted auburn bob out of place) stands next to her husband in a freshly pressed crimson designer suit. One diamond-laden hand rests reassuringly on the Politician's forearm, and the other clutches a white lace-trimmed monogrammed handkerchief. The once proud figure that was always at the forefront of important issues like police brutality, affirmative action, and inner-city poverty removes a piece of paper with prepared remarks from his suit jacket pocket. This is surprising to many in the room since he's known for his eloquent, and often rhythmic, off-the-cuff Southern preacher speaking style. But today, he needs a script. The room grows quiet as the crowd of jackals leans in, tape recorders thrust into the air, camera lenses train like laser beams on the podium to capture every single word (grammatical errors and all) and facial tics for the six o'clock news, morning edition of the paper, and wire services. The Politician clears his throat. They move in for the kill.

And then—always in the same order—he says it.

He's betrayed his family, his beautiful wife of some ungodly number of years, his sainted mother who worked three jobs to put him through college, and most of all the black community by indulging in one of four things (if it's more than two things, then the press conference is replaced by a short segment on *Inside Edition*): drugs, an affair (sometimes resulting in a child), money laundering or embezzlement— or both. After this painful admission, the Wife closes her eyes and lets a single tear drop from her eyes. She dabs at it delicately with the handkerchief and loops her arm through her husband's, propping up his sagging frame. The minister holds his dog-eared King James Bible in one hand, shakes his head, and pats the Politician on the shoulder, murmuring softly for support, "God forgives." The Politician never cries at these press conferences. "I'm sorry," he says with all the sincerity he can muster.

And then, instead of hastily departing from the hotel and slinking off to some small town you can't find on a map, never to be heard from again, he looks straight into the cameras and pounds the podium for emphasis and says it.

"I'm the real victim here." He and his poor family were set up by "the man."

Pandemonium erupts in the ballroom as the reporters look on in shock and disbelief.

Suddenly the Politician straightens up to his just-shy-of-six-feet height. He's magically morphed into the proud man he once was. His eyes no longer look like they are red from crying; they flash with righteous indignation. His chest puffs up, filling out the expensive suit. The Wife straightens up too, diamonds from her rings and broach glint off the lights from the cameras. The minister begins to rock back and forth, humming "God Is Not Through with Me Yet" under his breath. The Politician crumples up the tear-stained speech, casts it aside, and begins a 27.5-minute rant about

how the FBI wiretaps and paid informants are just pawns in
the government's ongoing campaign to discredit his name,
destroy his family, and distract him from continuing his no-
ble and lifesaving work as the spokesman for black America.
As the reporters scribble down his comments furiously, he
announces that his trusted adviser, the minister, is rallying a
national movement of preachers and deacons from around
the country in support of his tarnished reputation. In just
under an hour, the Politician has gone from fallen hero to
born-again martyr.

And what do black folks do? We support the Politician
and vilify any black person who cooperated in the investigation. Ignoring the wiretaps, grainy photographs, and DNA
tests, we mutter, "The man's always out to bring a brother
down. Forget the indiscretions, lies, and out-and-out thiev-
ery. That traitor is an Uncle Tom. We won't let 'The Man'
tell us who are leaders are." Say what?!

Now we're not saying that "The Man" isn't out to get
any and all of us. Let's be clear: We know full well that there
are racist forces working tirelessly to bring down our leaders
and regular black folks every day. But what we are saying is
that these politicians, music icons, sports figures, and self-
appointed leaders should stop giving them so much made-
for-a-TV-movie material to work with! Stop getting caught
out there with your pants down. Stop having affairs, stealing
money, and using drugs. In other words: Just say No!

* * *

We should all take a page from the example set by our patron saint for this chapter, Anita Hill. The world was riveted in 1991 when a soft-spoken University of Oklahoma law professor stepped forward and told the world that then Supreme Court nominee Clarence Thomas had sexually harassed her when she once worked with him. Our community was torn. Who was this black woman alleging these horrible things against this black nominee? Could Thomas have done the things she said? Is Thomas lying? And if he had done these things, was it worth risking not having a black justice on the highest court in the nation?

Hill's personal business was reported in national and international outlets. Her anguished family members were also subjected to media scrutiny and dragged into a three-ring circus televised for weeks. Dignified and composed throughout the hearings, Hill withstood countless hours of testimony, disrespectful and sexist lines of questioning from senators, and was basically called a liar.

To refute the charges, Thomas's position was the classic scandal-diffusing defense: he called the panel's inquisition a "high-tech lynching." Playing the race card, Thomas effectively took the credibility out of Hill's claims. The senators were afraid of being labeled racists and immediately backed off. Suddenly Hill became the target of the panel's investigation.

And while Thomas was eventually confirmed, we respect

Hill for taking the unpopular road and having the courage to stand up for herself and women everywhere.

As such, we think ABWs should take Hill's lead and follow the words from the title of her book, *Speaking Truth to Power*.

The ABW's Top 5 Ways to Speak Truth to Power

Whether it's the disgraced politician caught embezzling funds from a government agency or the music legend charged with statutory rape, as black women we need to take the lead and stop supporting those people who do not support our interests. Our issues are too pressing, our needs too great, our dollars too important. We can't have people who are easily distracted to represent us or line the pockets of entertainers who commit illegal acts. We're not saying they need to be perfect, but shouldn't they be expected not to break the law? The only way to stop our leaders, politicians, and entertainers from doing these things is to stop forgiving them for these indiscretions and hold them accountable for betraying our trust. The following is the ABW plan of action to speak truth to power:

1. **Keep your money in your pocket.** What do you think would happen if the next time (and goodness knows

there's going to be a next time) a black politician or artist got caught doing something scandalous we took a stand with our wallets? Don't show up at the fish fry to raise money for his legal defense fund. Stop buying his latest CD. Don't call your local radio station to request his oversexed lyrics. Like the saying goes, money talks. And when these people start seeing that black women aren't supporting them or their projects financially, they'll start taking notice.

2. **Don't believe the hype.** Many times after suffering a fall from grace, these clowns try to flip the script and come back on the scene. The mainstream conservative suddenly adopts Afrocentric principles, trades in the three-piece suits for a two-piece kente cloth outfit and a kufi. The singer tries to release a gospel single to plead his case. Don't believe that these leopards can change their spots.

3. **Get involved.** The only way that you can get a new political agenda going is to vote in new blood. Do some research on new politicians, attend local events, and see what they're talking about. Finally, volunteer. Don't expect things to be different unless you're willing to do some work to help things change.

4. **Spread the word.** As ABWs, we love any opportunity to run our mouths, so educate your friends and family mem-

bers on these important issues. Encourage them to throw away the albums of any disgraced artist and encourage them not to buy the latest one. Tell them that they don't have to accept the status quo and that there are different options out there. Each one can teach one.

5. **Step up to the plate.** Believe in something deeply? Then there's no reason that you can't run for office and effect change. As evidenced by all the women cited in Chapter 3, "A History Lesson," sometimes the best man for the job is an angry black woman.

And please don't get us wrong, it's not only the prominent, so-called role models that keep us down. The sad reality is that the majority of the damage to the public and private image of blacks is done on a daily basis by normal, everyday black people who simply refuse to act right. We're even willing to go so far as to pray that they don't know any better, but if you had a black mother like we had black mothers, you know that's a reach.

So whether it's the nasty coworker who makes it her business to remind you that you're never going to be good enough for a promotion or the extra-loud-talking, unruly, ridiculous-looking individual who continuously shows up on the eleven o'clock news in her house slippers, pink rollers, and crusted-over eyes talking 'bout, "I seen it all from my back window!" you don't have to be mad at yourself for

cringing in embarrassment and wishing you were invisible—
you're not alone. Not that we're advocating the permanent
disassociation so many of us privately pray for at times like
these, we're simply going to give you a couple of tips on
how to stay cool in the middle of the heat.

1. **Physically remove yourself from the situation.** Al-
   though at the time it may seem like an unnecessary incon-
   venience, sometimes it's better to walk away rather than
   allow them to continue aggravating your spirit with their
   antics. Use this opportunity to hit them with the "I know
   your mother taught you better than this" look.

2. **Take a temporary break from the race.** In instances
   where you're trapped with the offending party—like, say,
   on a bus ride—consider yourself an honorary white woman.
   Continually remind yourself that you have nothing to do
   with whatever they're going through. In fact, you're just
   as appalled as Buffy, Cindy, and their clique of bleached
   blondes.

3. **Help your sister out.** Kindly pull her aside for a non-
   judgmental, one-on-one, "I'm just trying to help you
   out" chat. Explain to her that small areas in business envi-
   ronments are never a good place to discuss personal issues. At the end of the day, maybe LaShonda didn't
   realize that the entire elevator was listening to her blow-

by-blow recap of last night's booty call—and she might even thank you for the heads-up. Caution: You should only do this in cases of familiarity. If you step to the wrong LaShonda on the right day, you might just catch a bad one.

4. **Hit them with the classic black mama "don't make me come over there" look.** Sometimes a simple glance is worth a thousand words. Make brief but stern eye contact, and immediately resume what you were doing. No words needed; raised eyebrows and turned-up nose a bonus. Hey, it stopped us dead in our tracks when we wanted to play like we didn't know any better.

5. **Check yourself.** We all are prone to the blackout, being a little overzealous around our folks, or simply being extra hype. So the next time you feel the need to curse out whoever just disrespected you in public at the top of your voice or carry on like you and your friends are the only ones in the room, pause, count to ten, and remember you're simply better than that, and keep it moving.

7

in Love and War: Black Men and ABWs

Before we begin this chapter, we'd like to set the record straight: This is not going to be the new millennium "black men ain't s&*%" diatribe. ABWs love them some black men. Deeply. They're our confidants, they're our protectors, they're our brothers in the struggle—the ones that we turn to when the world has let us down. And the loving? Girls, don't even get us started on how good it is when a brother is putting in serious work between the sheets—he'll have us sweating out our perm just to lie in his arms a little longer. Despite all the stereotypes and rants and scary six o'clock news stories that make it clear it's black men against the world, no one will ever love them stronger—and more unconditionally—than us black women. The proof: We've written countless award-winning songs, best-selling books, renown poems, passionate love letters, earnest haiku, provocative movie scripts, and tear-stained diary entries about them. Cried countless tears of joy, ecstasy, and sometimes pain over them. Even lost our natural minds for them.

And don't let him be a good one: He'll have us lying to our mamas, standing up our friends on girls' night, calling in sick on the job (knowing we need the extra hours), ruining our good credit report, running up our phone, heat, and electric bills, co-signing for cars and cell phones, putting his debts into our name, letting him hold our ride while we're riding the bus, and slapboxing in the street with any woman who dares to step to him. Because ABWs go hard for our men.

Of course, on the flip side of this love connection is this: Don't nobody, and we mean nobody, know how to jump on, pluck, work, twist, or twirl our last good nerve like a black man. He knows it like no other because he was raised by a black woman, so he's got firsthand working knowledge of our hot buttons and pressure points. And, as a result, he's got a Ph.D. in getting us fired up.

Our patron saint for this chapter, Erykah Badu, knows what we're talking about. In fact, she wrote a hugely popular and hilarious song about it. "Tyrone," her finger-popping, sing-along-with-your-hands-on-your-hips single, chronicled a relationship gone tragically south after she realized her man wasn't ever going to get it together. Brotherman didn't have any money, wasn't looking for a job, was surrounded by broke friends, and, most importantly, had a severe lack of respect for their relationship. Simply put: He wasn't invested in her or handling his business. So she politely informed him that his services were no longer required and that he should call his boy, Tyrone, to help him come get his shit. And no, he couldn't use her phone to make that call. Sisters everywhere instantly related to this track. When it came on, we all jumped to our feet and sang along in solidarity, nodding knowingly at each other, mouthing the lyrics to boyfriends on their way out of the picture. Gentleman, you betta call Tyrone. It was a 1990s update on the Aretha Franklin classic "R-E-S-P-E-C-T." Erykah put on blast a whole host of men that all of us have dated at some point in our lives (and if you say you haven't dated this guy, then you're probably dating him right now!).

But what's an ABW to do if she loves her man and wants to work things out? Goodness knows, we're the work-it-out queens—always willing to empathize, rationalize, and talk it out for the umpteenth time. You know, give him a first, second, third, twentieth chance. To help you better navigate the rough patches that will inevitably creep up in your relationship, we put together these survival tips to keep you out of jail, avoid a restraining order, out of the mouths of the church gossip, employed, with halfway decent credit—and, best of all, with your man.

The Quiz

Want to know what type of man you are dealing with? Have him take our quiz and then check his answers against our key to see if your relationship is salvageable or if you should tell him to call Tyrone.

1. After coming home from a hard day at work, you stumble into the living room and kick off your shoes. Your man:

   A. Asks you to keep it down because he's trying to watch ESPN *SportsCenter*.
   B. Immediately turns off the TV and rubs your feet until you fall asleep on the sofa.
   C. Tells you about how much his day sucked also and asks if you feel like cooking dinner.

2. You've been dropping hints all week about a beautiful blouse in the window of your favorite boutique. Then, on your birthday, your man presents you with:

   A. The flat-screen TV he wanted for his birthday, explaining that he got it so you guys could spend more quality time watching *SportsCenter* together.
   B. Not only the beautiful blouse, but also a matching skirt.
   C. Λ blouse from a store you've never heard of.

3. While out to dinner at your favorite restaurant, an attractive woman keeps throwing suggestive glances in your man's direction. When you comment on her inappropriate behavior, he:

   A. Slips her his number when you leave the table to go to the ladies' room to check your makeup.
   B. Ignores her throughout the meal and makes a point of putting his arm around you as you walk by her table as you leave the restaurant.
   C. Tells you that you can't really blame the woman for being unable to stop herself from checking out such a fine brother.

4. There's a scheduling conflict: Your man wants to invite his friends over to the house to watch the NBA draft on the same night as your book club dinner. He:

   A. Won't even entertain a discussion about making alternate arrangements and invites his friends over, against your wishes.
   B. Makes alternate plans to watch the draft at another friend's house.
   C. Sits around the house in his underwear in the living room watching the draft by himself.

5. Your car payment is overdue and you're running a little short this month, so you have to ask your man for a little help. He:

A. Says, "Even though I drive it all the time, that's not my ride. Hope you got enough money for the bus."
B. Surprises you by making not only one payment but two payments so you can get a chance to get on your financial feet.
C. Says he'll loan you the money at the going interest rate.

The Answer Key

If your man scored mostly A's:

This will come as no surprise to you or any of your girlfriends who keep telling you that your man is no good. He's so bad, you've probably had his boy Tyrone on speed dial in your cell phone, home phone, and work phone (and e-mail and two-way pager number) since day one of the relationship for every time he shows out. And goodness knows, he loves to show out. This type of man doesn't change, and he's showing you exactly how trifling he is every chance he gets. Call Tyrone and move on.

If your man scored mostly B's:

Congratulations! We've got good news: You've found the One. He's a great catch and clearly has only you and your happiness on his mind. He appreciates your ABW spirit and respects you. Treat him right. And don't worry, you'll never need to call Tyrone with Mr. Right, because a man as good as him doesn't even hang around losers like Tyrone.

If your man scored mostly C's:

This is the type of man that most of us end up with. He's really tricky to read and hard to classify because sometimes he appears like he's insensitive to your needs but will never directly hurt your feelings. You will find it difficult to get really mad at him because he never really gets out of bounds. Save Tyrone's number should the need arise, and tread lightly.

Now that we've classified the type of man you're dealing with, read on to find out what type of relationship land mines you'll be facing and how to escape unscathed.

The Top Things Black Men Say That Can Cause Mass Destruction of the Relationship and Your Mind

Yellow Alert: Questions that, while annoying, shouldn't be seen as a serious sanity-threatening situation.

- "You wearing that?"
- "What's up with your hair?"
- "You 'sleep?"

- "You know I love you, right?"
- "Can you lemme hold a couple of dollars?"
- "Is the baby crying?"
- "You know, my mom said . . ."
- "My boy said his girl does it, and he said she liked it . . ."

Orange Alert: Man your verbal battle stations, ladies, because your honey has launched a serious but not deadly assault on your sanity.

- "Didn't I tell you before? . . ."
- "You didn't get the message I left you?"
- "Why?"
- "Do I have to go?"
- "I'll be right back."
- "Forget you then/Whatever."
- "I quit my job today."

Red Alert: There's no way around this one: You're in a DEFCON 1 situation. Your sanity cannot be saved. There's about to be a blackout.

- "I don't know her/I don't know how she got my number."
- "It wasn't me."
- "See, what had happened was . . ."

- "Are you going to let that girl come between what we have?"
- "She don't mean nothin' to me."

The ABW Plan of Action: How to Save Your Relationship and Your Sanity

Dealing with a Yellow-Level Offense: We like to call these offenses the Fast Flash because these infuriating questions are almost always asked by men in a hurried fashion as to not completely arouse your suspicion or illicit a sting-ing counter verbal attack (beware though: it's a good ploy for them to use when asking for money). Most of the time these insensitive questions are uttered in passing on the way out the door, on the way to the bathroom, during a commercial break, just as you're about to fall into REM sleep, or on the phone (outside immediate striking distance). These are the comments that make you say, "No, he didn't just ask me/say that to me." Well, girlfriend, yes he did. And chances are he'll say it again, unless you nip it in the bud quickly.

Luckily, these offenses usually don't require a verbal response. A strategic eye roll, a sharp sucked tooth and a sigh, or simply turning your back will shut the situation down and cause the enemy to retreat and ponder his mistakes. If the question is about your appearance, though, you might have to break from the nonverbal communication pattern by muttering under your breath with gritted teeth to send a clear message. Try something along the lines of, "No, he didn't just ask me [fill in the blank with his inappropriate comment about your appearance]." For some reason, men have a difficult time realizing that unless they are licensed hairstylists with at least two notable celebrity clients or fashion designers with a collection selling at Macy's and Nordstrom, then they should keep any and all negative or questioning comments about your hair—including style, length, color, and texture—as well as wardrobe, accessory, and shoe selection to themselves. Like Momma always said: If you don't have something nice to say, don't say anything at all.

If you're extremely lucky, he's really good at reading nonverbal cues and will learn from this encounter and plan accordingly in the future. Unfortunately, we don't know many men that learn from these mistakes. They seem to like playing with fire and will continue to test you. Yellow-level offenses can escalate into more dangerous situations—sometimes causing you to reassess the threat level and change the offense level—when two or more are launched in a short period of time. If your man commits a double yellow offense—such as saying, "I know I'm late for dinner with your boss but what had happened was . . ."—get ready to rumble. Another thing that can cause this situation to escalate quickly is if these questions are asked in front of company, coworkers, or his boys.

Dealing with an Orange-Level Offense: Your situation just got a bit more serious, but there probably won't be any tears shed (his), bloodshed (again, his), or blackouts (all you, girl). These comments also seem innocent enough on the surface, but a smart ABW isn't easily fooled. Most likely these sorry statements will be an attempt to cover up some sort of missed appointment or a halfhearted attempt to get out of a social commitment. Most likely you will end up having a heated discussion to explain to your man that he's stepped out of bounds and needs to retreat immediately.

Deal with the low-pressure points like when he clearly overlooked or chose to "forget" a social commitment by questioning his whereabouts and explaining how much this appointment meant to you. This "discussion" may most likely take place with elevated voice levels so you should try to secure the perimeter and make sure there are no witnesses (usually it's only red-level offenses that allow you to put your business out in the street). If you must shut down the situation in public, fire off a razor-sharp retort in the presence of company (if this comment occurs in front of his boys, then you've scored a direct hit).

The boiling point comes in stability-threatening offenses like "I quit my job." Now, admittedly, this is a rare one.

Most black men with the good sense God gave them aren't going to just up and quit a j-o-b without having another one lined up for fear of losing his place at the dinner table and incurring your wrath with a serious show of force. But if your man does decide he's in the market for a change, remain calm. Ask him to fully explain (this is the part where he should break out presentation materials with charts and graphs) why half of the household is out of work and exactly what his twenty-four–hour plan is to secure gainful employment. Clearly, securing employment prior to this discussion is the *only* way to diffuse the situation immediately and avoid a deadly show of force.

The other dangerous comment is the casually launched "whatever then" to some point you've tried to make or question you've asked. Nothing enrages an ABW more than the thought that she's being ignored or taken for granted. We often flashback to an unforgettable movie when this happens in our relationships. Remember the Glenn Close character in *Fatal Attraction* when she maniacally tells her panicked lover that she "won't be ignored" after he tries to end their clandestine affair? That's one of the best lines to use in this situation. Look your man straight in the eye, take a deep breath, and in your best scorned lover/psycho babe voice say, "I won't be ignored." While he won't necessarily remember the exact scene from the movie, the deadly calm sound of your voice as you make this statement is sure to provoke the desired reaction. This line is guaranteed to send chills up your man's spine. And you don't even have to boil a rabbit!

Dealing with a Red-Level Offense: Red-level offenses are labeled as such because as soon as he makes these pitiful statements, all you can see is red. Your blood is boiling, fists are clenched, and the pressure in your head is mounting quickly. These incendiary comments are a clear and present danger to your sanity because they are always a lie relating to another woman.

When it comes to the thought of our man and another woman, all ability to rationalize flies out of the window. It's the most serious violation and therefore must be treated as such. After you send the children to their room, excuse yourself from your friends or ask your company to leave, and seek cover to assess your strategy. It's about to go down. There are few rules when dealing with this situation because in most cases you will lose control of your ability to process rational thought, speak intelligently, and control your limbs (removal of sharp objects is always wise).

What you have to do is assess quickly what the end result of this squirmish is going to be. Do you believe there's a possibility that your man isn't lying and that you can salvage the relationship, or has he been caught with his hand in another woman's cookie jar? You may have to call in reinforcements. If there is absolutely no way that you can possibly stay with this man, then follow these steps to get back to the loving ABW you're capable of being.

1. Get your girl—the one who will get up out her bed at exactly 3:01 A.M., hop in her ride, come pick you up, and drive you over to ol' what's-her-name's house to see if his car is there, and then stand dutifully while you key it if he is—and keep all your early-morning activities to herself. She's going to be extremely useful as you plot his demise.

2. Have a good cry on her shoulder. It's good for the soul to show some emotion, particularly when your feelings have been hurt.

3. Seek and destroy (see details in step #1).

4. Go home and get a good night's sleep.

5. Get up, get dressed in your finest come-hither outfit, get your hair done, put on some M•A•C lipglass, some sweet-smelling perfume, and your game face, and get you a new man.

8

OUR KIDS: LABOR WAS THE EASY PART

We're duped from the beginning: For nine months, we go through the motion of carrying a human being in our body while our friends and family fill our heads with delusions of how great motherhood is going to be. Of course, we fall for it. And when the doctor places our little bundles of joy into our arms, we instantly fall hopelessly in love with these fascinating little creatures—their smell, their perfect little toes, the cooing, the promise of a lifetime of unconditional love. And then . . . they make their first bowel movement. And they cry all night long. They tell you no. They get sick and throw up all over your new silk suit—at 7:45 A.M., as you're rushing to catch the 8:00 A.M. train to your boss's mandatory staff meeting. They effortlessly take you to depths of embarrassment that you never thought you'd see in your child—all the while proclaiming to love you.

For sure, children are gifts from God—but they can also seem like double agents in the devil's army. And during the duration of raising a child, there will inevitably be moments where you wish God would have just sent you some money in a card and kept junior for himself. Alas, the latter is not possible—so you have to figure out how to raise your child and maintain your sanity while avoiding a visit from an agent from Child Protective Services.

This is by no means easy.

But our patron saint Claire Huxtable sure made it seem that way, huh? A partner at a prestigious law firm, she effortlessly raised five children while maintaining an immaculate Brooklyn brownstone and cooking three meals per day. She truly was the epitome of every woman—she participated in school functions, doled out sage advice to anyone who needed it, and was never too tired for Cliff. God bless Claire Huxtable.

Needless to say, she messed it up for all of us. Clearly, she was but a TV character, because no woman in her right mind can juggle that much responsibility and still manage to keep a smile on her—and her husband's—face. And look fly doing it. For those of us who exist in real time, there are always going to be situations that try our last nerve, or cause us to rue the day we ever laid eyes on our baby's daddy. Just remember: You really, really, really do love the kids.

Want to know what type of child you're dealing with?

Have your kids take this quiz and then check their answers against our key to determine what type of trickery and foolishness you are going to face during these wonder years they call childhood.

The Quiz

1. When your mother comes home from a long day at the office to find the house looking like a cyclone ripped through the living room, you:

   A. Lie with a perfectly straight face and tell her you just got home from school yourself and that your little brother must have done all of this.
   B. Immediately explain how you were in the midst of cleaning up and thought that the best way to get started was to pull everything out into the middle of the floor.
   C. Apologize profusely and begin to clean up immediately.

2. It's Mother's Day so you thought the best way to show your appreciation for your mother's love and support is to:

A. Write your name on the card that your thoughtful sister bought and take credit for the gift she made in school.

B. Quickly grab a bunch of old pictures of your mother and put together a homemade scrapbook called "This is your life, Mom."

C. Let her sleep in, prepare her breakfast in bed, and present her with a store-wrapped gift.

3. Dying for the new $200 leather sports team jacket that all the cool kids are sporting at school, you:

A. Tell your mom that unfortunately your only coat was stolen from your locker with the hopes that she'll take you to the store and buy you the expensive leather coat.

B. Tell your mom that your new coat isn't keeping you very warm and ask if she would buy you a new one so you don't catch a cold.

C. Keep your desire for the expensive jacket to yourself because you know that $200 is too much to spend on a jacket, especially since you've already got a perfectly good coat in your closet.

4. You're hanging out with your friends on a Friday night and as your eleven o'clock curfew approaches, one of your

friends suggests that the group hop in their cars and head over to a party on the other side of town. You:

A. Go to the party and when you get home you climb through the bedroom window that you conveniently left open and slip into your bed undetected.

B. Go to the party but call your mom first and tell her that the friend you rode with got a flat tire and that you should be home in about an hour.

C. Head home. You'll get the details on the party tomorrow.

5. You fail your French midterm and are required to have your mother sign the test and return it to your teacher. You:

A. Change the "F" to a "B" and accept your mother's heaping praise and offer to prepare your favorite dinner after you present it proudly to her for her signature.

B. Deciding there's no need to upset her with such distressing news regarding your academic shortcomings, you have your best friend forge her signature and turn the test into your teacher the next day.

C. Give the test to your mother for her signature, promise to study harder, and give yourself a punishment until you bring your grades up.

The Answer Key

For each "A," give yourself 8 points.
For each "B," give yourself 4 points.
For each "C," give yourself 1 point.

If your child scored more than 29 points, you're in trouble, ABW mom—your child is a bad ass with a tendency to do dumb stuff. He will test your patience until the day he leaves your house. On the plus side, though, he's not the brightest bulb when it comes to trying to get away with stuff, so there will be plenty of opportunities to catch him in blatant lies and half-truths. Keep him on a short leash, stay on your toes, and always double-check his answers and whereabouts. He's easily influenced by his friends, which will cause him significant drama. The good news is that you two will probably share a lot of quality time together as he will most likely spend much of his teenage years on punishment.

If your child scored between 12 and 19, you may want to sit down for this, because there's really no way to say this nicely: Your child is basically the devil's spawn. The problem with this child is that he thinks he's slicker than he actually is. His personal creed is: "What my mom doesn't know won't hurt me." He convinces himself that he's sparing you hurt by not divulging all the details about any given situation and considers it a personal achievement to get over on people. This type of child will work your last—and we do mean *last*—good nerve until the day he leaves your house (and hopefully he won't be leaving it to enter into a witness protection program).

If your child scored under 11 points, don't get excited—he's probably bad, too. Yes, he picked all the "good kid" answers, but your child is no saint. In fact, you're probably in the biggest trouble of all, because if your kid tried to get you to believe that, if faced with the above scenarios, he would choose "C," then he's most likely one of the other children mentioned in the "A" and "B" sections. Read them closely.

So now that you know what type of child you're dealing with, here are a few scenarios you are bound to face while raising your precious offspring and some new parenting tools to help you keep at least some of your sanity.

1. The scenario:

After you told your daughters 50 million times not to play with their prized hula hoop in the house, you come home from a long day of work only to find that in the midst of a hula-hooping contest, someone managed to hula right into the middle of your prized and extremely expensive glass coffee table.

Initial reaction:
Pass out from shock, and, after realizing no one was hurt, run down to the computer, log on, and post both of the kids on eBay.

What an ABW should do:
Assess the situation and make sure no one was hurt. Calmly tell the children to go to their rooms so you can clean up the mess. Take your time cleaning up the mess—this draws out the anxiety in the kids, who should be upstairs preparing to meet their maker and praying to the Lord that, whatever happens, the punishment be swift. Then go down to the basement, find the biggest box you can, open the door, place the box inside, and quietly ask them to place every last toy they own in the box, because they are going to be given to a child in need who listens to their mother.

2. The scenario:
Despite years of good behavior training and the preemptive "we're going to the store" cautionary speech, within moments of arriving to the store they proceed to scream, pull everything within arm's reach off the shelves, and cut a fool.

Initial reaction:

Snatch them up under one armpit, leaving them dangling with at least one foot off the ground, and snarl from between clenched teeth, "Don't you know who I am? I am the alpha and the omega. I will *hurt* you."

What an ABW should do:

When possible, be sure that your child is adequately rested before heading out for the store. Minimize your shopping time by being prepared with knowledge of everything that you're looking for. Bring something small that they may entertain themselves with for at least half of the time that you're going to be there. If they still insist on showing their true colors, immediately attempt to have a calm but stern intervention conversation, involving bribery and barter (if you let Mommy finish grocery shopping, I'll get you the cookies with the sprinkles on them and let you eat them on the way home). When all else fails, accept defeat gracefully and live to shop another day when little Mikey is at his grandma's house.

3. The scenario:

Your teen is caught at the neighbor's house/school/church doing something he's not supposed to be doing—smoking, kissing, playing with fire.

Initial reaction:
Smack fire out of his mouth and ask him if he feels like
    putting cigarettes/tongues/anything-under-the-damn-
    sun in his mouth now.

What an ABW should do:
In addition to swift and severe punishment, make him
    volunteer at a local hospice or hospital where he can see
    the effects of AIDS, lung cancer, arson victims, etc.,
    firsthand.

4. The scenario:
Your baby is extra cranky and can't seem to stop fussing
and whining—she doesn't want a bottle, doesn't want to
be held, and sure doesn't want to be put down. She just
won't be quiet.

Initial reaction:
Pack up her stuff and put her on the doorstep of whoever
    the hell told you this parenting thing was going to be a
    good idea.

What an ABW should do:
After you check to make sure that your baby is not ill, not
    wet, and not hungry, understand that you're not in
    control. You're not doing anything wrong—babies cry.

So take a deep breath, put the baby down somewhere safe, and call for reinforcements—the baby's father, a close friend, relative, or even professional baby-sitter who will empathize and provide you with a grown folk time-out.

5. The scenario:

After asking your daughter to pick up her shoes from the middle of the floor for the umpteenth time, she mumbles something unintelligible under her breath, rolls her eyes, and sighs before finally bending over and doing what you asked her to do forty minutes ago.

Initial reaction:

Grab one of those shoes and clock her right upside the head and ask her if she had something else she needed to say.

What an ABW should do:

Tell her that if she's got so much she wants to say to you, the two of you will be spending a lot more time in the house over the next two months talking about all the things she clearly has on her mind.

Top 20 Rhetorical ABW Mom Questions

Explain to your children that these questions do not require an answer. The appropriate response is to shut your mouth, stop whatever you're doing, maintain eye contact in a respectful and humble manner, and do whatever you can to bring me back to my former, pleasant, Claire Huxtable demeanor. If all else fails, they should probably seek secure shelter and the protection of an adult.

1. Do you want me to come up there?

2. Do you want me to pull this car over?

3. Do you need me to call your father?

4. Don't you hear me talking to you?

5. Do you want me to give you something to cry about?

6. You do remember I told you not to do that, right?

7. Have you lost your mind?

8. What did I tell you?

9. Do you think I won't embarrass you in front of your little friends?

10. Who do you think you are?

11. Who do you think you're talking to?

12. Do you still want to live in this house?

13. You think you're grown, right?

14. Did I ask you what you thought?

15. So you're the official class clown, huh?

16. If all your friends jumped off a bridge, would you do it too?

17. How many times do I have to tell you _____? (Fill in the blank.)

18. Do I look stupid to you?

19. Do you think money grows on trees?

20. Who's the parent here—you or me?

TOP 5 THINGS YOUR KIDS SAY TO YOU TO CAUSE A BLACKOUT

The power of words is always underestimated—the slightest things said can send an ABW over the edge.

1. Daddy said I could.

2. So? Whatever!

3. It wasn't me.

4. But I thought . . .

5. No.

TOP 5 THINGS YOUR KIDS SHOULD NEVER DO WHEN THEY'RE ABOUT TO GET IT

Your child's been caught—time to dole out punishment. We know this hurts you more than it hurts them, so here's a couple of ways you can help them make it easier on themselves.

1. Run: It's only going to make us more angry if we have to sweat our hair out.

2. Tell Grandma: She can't save you.

3. Threaten to call child services: Idle threats will only lead to a real reason for them to come get you.

4. Say, "I don't love you": We know you don't mean it, but it still hurts.

5. Start crying before we even do anything to you: It will just irritate us even more.

Top 5 Signs an ABW is About to Lose Total Control

After the fact, it's hard to pinpoint the exact moment you lost control. We've got you covered! You know your child's clearly crossed the line when you:

1. Count to ten with your eyes closed.

2. Grab your Bible and turn to your favorite passage.

3. Start looking for extension cords, belts, switches, slippers . . .

4. Start locking the doors, pulling down the shades, and unplugging the phones.

5. Dial 911 and tell the operator, "Hold on—you might want to send someone over shortly."

9

The BLACKOUT: WhaT YOU ShOULD NeVeR SaY To an ABW

There are but a few things that can cause an ABW to totally lose control. Sure, there's the occasional outburst or curse-out, but a total loss of control by an ABW is rare. But when it happens, everyone should take cover. We like to classify the total unadulterated loss of control as a *blackout*. She may unleash a torrent of stinging words or destroy or eliminate property depending on the offense. It's almost akin to an actual electrical blackout, as its victims are temporarily powerless and paralyzed with fear. Rare in occurrence, they are often talked about by coworkers, family members, and loved ones in hushed tones. Some blackouts have reached mythical proportions in offices or nightclubs like a Big Foot or UFO sighting.

It's hard to get ABWs to talk about their blackout experiences. For those who have blacked out on people, they will tell you they don't remember much about the experience. There's no longer a concept of place, time, or proper conduct. It's like an out-of-body experience. Oftentimes, when an ABW comes out of the blackout, she's tired and can't remember specifically what she's said or to whom. She may need to rest and will most likely, due to the rapid rate of speech, require several glasses of water. She usually has to rely on the eyewitness testimony of others to recount what happened.

The patron saint of the blackout is the character Bernadine in Terry McMillan's *Waiting to Exhale*. In both the hugely popular book and film (Angela Bassett played the hell out of this part on the big screen), Bernadine blacks out after her husband informs her on New Year's Eve that he is leaving her and their two children after several years of marriage. Consumed by what can only be described as a blinding, murderous rage, Bernadine races through her house and rips thousands of dollars of expensive clothing off the hangers, loads it with all of his treasured collectibles into his BMW, and sets it all ablaze. In a more lucid state of blackout, she sells all his belongings, including golf clubs, expensive ski equipment, and personal affects at a "Love's Hangover" garage sale, where everything—his super-expensive skis, his art collection, his drawers—is tagged at one dollar.

So how should your friends, coworkers, family members, and boyfriends avoid witnessing you blacking out on them?

Pass along this list of things they should never say to keep everyone (property included) safe.

5 Things Men Should Never Say To Avoid The Blackout

1. "I only slept with her once."

2. "I crashed your car."

3. "You gaining weight?"

4. "How do I know that kid is mine?"

5. "I went to the clinic today . . ."

5 Things Coworkers Should Never Say To Avoid The Blackout

1. "We've going to have to make some cuts."

2. "You only got this job because of affirmative action."

3. "I need to talk to you about a complaint."

4. "I'm reporting you to your manager."

5. "I'm going to need you to come in on Saturday."

5 Things Your Kids Should Never Say To Avoid The Blackout

1. "My girlfriend is pregnant," or "I'm pregnant."

2. "It's not mine—I swear!"

3. "I need you to bail me out."

4. "You're not the boss of me."

5. "So? I don't care."

5 Things Your Friends Should Never Say To Avoid The Blackout

1. "I slept with your man, but he came on to me first."

2. "Don't call me anymore when your man dogs you out again."

3. "I'm sorry, I forgot to pick up your kids."

4. "You don't look as good as I do."

5. "I didn't know you didn't want me to tell your boyfriend you were out with someone else."

10 Signs The Blackout is Coming

If your friends don't memorize the above list, tell them to seek shelter if one or more of the following occur:

1. The removal of any jewelry or shoes

2. Asking children to go to their rooms and lock their doors

3. Quoting biblical passages

4. Removing breakable items

5. Clearing out desk drawers and all personal belongings from office

6. Testing the weight of heavy objects in her hands

7. Speaking in what sounds like profane tongues

8. Her head is actually spinning around on her neck

9. Starts a sentence with: "You know what? Let me tell you something . . ."

10. She throws a copy of this book at your head

10

OUR SISTERS IN THE STRUGGLE: ANGRY WHITE WOMEN

Yes, we do know how to give 'em hell and lay folks out for overstepping bounds, doing the opposite of what we say, getting on our nerves—breathing. But black women aren't the only ones who, with the curl of a lip and a serious glare, can send an errant misstepper into a tailspin. Indeed, there are some white women who've got the eye-roll/neck-swivel/curse-you-out-on-a-dare thing down damn near better than some of us sistahs. And we've got nothing but love for them!

Why? Because you've got to give it up to anyone who can not only stand up to an ABW, but hold her own against one. Admit it: Our image of white women has been painted—and tainted—with years of stereotypes of the white woman on a pedestal, her porcelain skin shielded by an expensive parasol, her dainty fingers wrapped around a fan, her bosom propped up by expensive material bought and paid for by her almighty white man. In our mind, she is quiet and blushingly shy— quick to defer, never, ever loud. Somewhat harmless and easily bullied if cornered by a *real* ABW with absolutely no fear of retribution.

So when she steps to us with the same fire, spirit, and "I don't give a damn" attitude best exemplified by us ABWs? Oh, she gets the keys to the ABW city—for being coura-geous, witty, quick on her feet, and willing to take one to the gut for her beliefs. And, true to the spirit of an ABW, angry white women (hereafter known as AWWs) have their own patron saint: Madonna. Come on now, be honest: That's one white woman who came as close as they come to being black without having at least one Tyrone somewhere in her family tree. She burst onto the scene in the 1980s, skirt all up her legs, fishnets askew, with beat-laced R&B songs that could hang on black radio stations—and an "I could care less about what you think of me" attitude that had white folks across the land wanting to kick her from the race. Of course, in true ABW fashion, Madonna didn't care what they thought because she was her own woman with her own style and completely against conforming to society's'stan-dards of white woman etiquette.

More recently, Madonna's gotten remarried, had a sec-ond child, and moved to England. But that fiery AWW is hard for her to hide, even harder to deny. Madonna is still one of us. Here, other notable AWWs who give us pause and make us proud:

Barbara Walters

Who she is: Celebrated journalist

Claim to fame: In 1976, she became the first female ever to anchor a news broadcast on a major network when she became a coanchor on *ABC Evening News* with Harry Reasoner. Today, she's clocking the highest salary ever paid a female journalist for her longtime TV news show, *20/20*, and her celebrated, high-profile celebrity specials.

Why she's an AWW: Bab's been well known for her ability to make the strongest people cry—both on and off the camera. She's extremely intelligent, and she doesn't suffer fools easily—and she's not afraid to throw you the Look if you remotely seem like you don't know what the hell you're talking about. Love her!

Martha Stewart

Who she is: Celebrated home guru

Claim to fame: After a failing career as a Wall Street stock broker, she started her own chichi catering company, building her business into a billion-dollar style conglomerate worshiped by millions of women looking for advice on how to cook, clean, and entertain to perfection.

Why she's an AWW: Legend has it that if you worked in the same building as Martha, you could hear her tearing into anyone who dared misstep. She's passionate about what she does, and anyone who can't perfect perfection gets told. She's our idol—and even as Martha loyalists turn on her as she deals with the insider trading mess, we've got her back—even if she ends up literally cleaning the big house.

Anna Wintour

Who she is: The fabulous editor in chief of the style bible, *Vogue*

Claim to fame: She climbed from the humble beginnings as a lowly fashion assistant at *Harper's Bazaar* in 1970 to the editor of *Vogue* by 1988—and she's sat high on her perch as the connoisseur of taste and fashion sense.

Why she's an AWW: Anyone who knows anything about fashion and *Vogue* knows that Anna doesn't play when it comes to making sure her workers are on point. So you dared to step your pretty little toes into the office sans Prada sandals? To the galleys with you! So sinister are her employee relation tactics that a former assistant wrote a book about it. The name? *The Devil Wears Prada*. Damn skippy!

Joan Rivers

Who she is: Comedienne and host of E! network's fashion reviews

Claim to fame: She reinvented herself on E! by becoming an arbiter of style—and a trasher of anyone who dared step onto the red carpet in anything she deemed completely not cute.

Why she's an AWW: Come on—her breakdown of celebrity red carpet style is priceless—stars who spend a whole lot of money to get all dolled up for the hottest awards shows literally break out in cold sweats as their publicists lead them over to Joan's mike. Why? Because they know she will c-l-o-w-n them to their face—and then make a whole show about it just one week later—putting hot Hollywood stylists out of work for years!

Sinead O'Connor

Who she is: Famed Irish singer

Claim to fame: One of the most distinctive and controversial pop stars of the 1990s who shaved her head, railed against everything from "The Star-Spangled Banner" to the Grammy Awards. Her most damaging act of defiance came when, at the end of a performance on *Saturday Night Live,* she ripped up a picture of the pope. Courtney Love and Alanis Morissette owe their careers to her for showing a pop star how to just wild out.

Why she's an AWW: She was always mad at something and didn't hesitate to use her mike to tell the world why she was pissed off. Most impressive was that she spoke her mind, no matter how damaging to her career it was to take a stand—she was even booed off the stage of Madison Square Garden after that pope incident—and still managed to be a revered singer.

Pink

Who she is: Famed R&B singer turned pop star

Claim to fame: She entered the music scene much like Madonna did—with strong R&B songs and a naughty-girl edge. We liked her because she seemed like she was a down chick, with her spiky pink hair, b-girl moves, and penchant for featuring good-looking black boys in her videos.

Why she's an AWW: She's since become more of a rocker

chick, but she's made the transition by kicking down the door and telling famed music exec LA Reid of all people what she was going to do with her career. The outcome? She managed to sings the songs that she wanted to sing—with a rocker flair—a move that got her noticed by mainstream pop lovers. And the girl actually wrote a song called "You Make Me Sick," in which she tells her man where he can get off—and in the video, she actually kicks his butt!

Ann Richards

Who she is: The first female governor of Texas

Claim to fame: She ran the hell out of the state of Texas, perhaps the most testosterone-laden, sexist state in the union. Best remembered for her line, "Poor George, he can't help it if he was born with a silver foot in his mouth!"

Why she's an AWW: She had no other choice in Texas, where the good ol' boys would cut her up and eat her like a fine piece of steak. Her acid tongue set her apart from other female legislators, who always seem to want to play nice. Not our girl, Ann. So bold was she that the official White House Web site describes her as "mannish" and "brash."

HILLARY RODHAM CLINTON

Who she is: U.S. senator and former first lady to our first black president, Bill Clinton

Claim to fame: Despite being massacred for saying early in her husband's administration that she didn't like to bake cookies and much preferred to help her man rule the world, she put her fingerprints all over the Clinton policies—and probably her husband's neck after she found out he'd cheated on her.

Why she's an AWW: Because she tightened Bill up over that whole Monica Lewinsky mess—in her autobiography, *Living History,* she says she wanted to "wring his neck" and refused to speak to him for weeks on end— and kept her man, under what we'd gather were some strict conditions—namely, no more interns. Stand by your man!

MARGARET THATCHER

Who she is: Prime minister of Britain

Claim to fame: She reigned in and ran Parliament with an iron fist and had the good ol' boys in the great U.S. of A. standing at attention.

Why she's an AWW: Have you ever seen British Parliament

in action? In order to even keep your head above water, you've got to come with the white politician's equivalent of the dozens. It's brutal up in there. Margaret not only ruled the same way a man would—with just enough finesse to remind everyone that she was a woman—she never backed down for the boys of Britain. To say she has quick wit with brains to match is an understatement. Back down? We don't think so.

Roseanne Barr

Who she is: Foul-mouthed comedienne/actress/former talk-show hostess

Claim to fame: She eloquently portrayed a wise-cracking, quick-witted white trash mom of three in her hit TV series, *Roseanne;* claimed to have multiple personalities and was extremely open about her obsession with plastic surgery and her inability to lose weight without going under the knife.

Why she's an AWW: She wouldn't hesitate to cut you up with her words—her tongue was more lethal than any knife she could carry. Do you want that rare or well done?

Joan Crawford

Who she is: Oscar-winning actress who helped put MGM Studios on the map

Claim to fame: She starred in dozens of movies, most notably her Oscar-winning turn in 1945's *Mildred Pierce,* and *Whatever Happened to Baby Jane?* She was later immortalized by a damaging biography turned film written by her adopted daughter Christina, who alleges to have been abused. We still cringe when we see wire hangers in our closet.

Why she was an AWW: Mama didn't take no mess. She actually retired from the business in 1974 after she saw a photograph of herself that she didn't like—and allegedly became a bitter old drunk who hadn't a problem cursing everybody out. Still, she was a glamour puss to the end—and evil to boot. She left only $77,000 of her $2 million estate to two of her four adopted children, and left nothing to Christina and little brother Christopher for "reasons known to them," as she so eloquently stated in her will. Now that's gangsta.

Arianna Huffington

Who she is: Famed syndicated columnist

Claim to fame: Her column, with a distinctly "I'll lay

you out" bent, is published in newspapers all across the country—and her face is a staple on the talking-head circuit. She's also a best-selling author. Her latest effort, *Fanatics & Fools,* sounds like something we could have written.

Why she's an AWW: If you've never seen this woman in action, check out some of the Sunday-morning political debate shows. She more than holds her own—in a loud, brash kind of way, with a Greek accent that leaves the talking heads in her wake. That she says exactly what's on her mind is a plus—that she doesn't give a damn if her politics don't make any sense is all the better. Put up your dukes!

Candace Bushnell

Who she is: Author whose column and book inspired our show *Sex and the City*

Claim to fame: Went from being New York's most celebrated single socialite/partygoer to being the ultimate tastemaker and how-to-date-well goddess. Inspired legions of women to step up their handbag and shoe game—and be happily single.

Why she's an AWW: She wasn't ashamed to talk about the sexual behavior that we all either secretly participate in or fantasize about—and is quick to cut up any man who missteps. And, to make things even hotter, she, at the age of forty-three, recently got married for the first time—to a ballet dancer ten years her junior who she knew for only a scant two months. You better work, Candace!

COURTNeY LOVe

Who she is: Completely out-of-control rock starlet

Claim to fame: She was married to now-deceased rock icon Kurt Cobain.

Why she's an AWW: *We're* afraid of her. Courtney routinely shows up to parties/celebrity events pissy drunk and ready to tell off anyone who looks at her halfway crooked. She hasn't had a hit in years, yet she strolls the red carpet like she's the hottest star out there—but her band Hole can pack a stadium faster than a New York minute, mainly because folks simply want to see what crazy antics she's gonna pull from her La Perla thong.

LOReNa BOBBiT

Who she is: The average Jane Schmo

Claim to fame: She chopped her husband's penis off with a knife after she found out he cheated on her one too many times.

Why she's an AWW: She put action behind her words. Need we say more?

TOP 10 WAYS YOU CAN TELL IF YOU'RE AN AWW

If you just aren't sure, but you think you might have some ABW tendencies, check out this list to see if you're a true AWW.

1. People are generally afraid to say anything remotely unpleasant to your face, for fear they'll get a good tongue-lashing.

2. You say exactly what's on your mind, without any regard for people's feelings.

3. People talk about you behind your back—and you don't give a damn.

4. You have nicknames like "Evilene" and "That Bitch."

5. ABWs don't scare you—at all.

6. You've heard of the "Glass Ceiling" but used your brass knuckles to smash right on through it.

7. Grown men cower at the mere mention of your name.

8. You've got your man in check—and he knows better than to step out of bounds because he can—and will— be replaced with a quickness.

9. Even in the face of severe public scrutiny and, at times, vilification, you still manage to keep your head up, handle your business, and force every last one of them to eat their words.

10. You recognize that we're all women—and that we're in this together.

11

Lights! Camera! Action!: An ABW's Favorite Movies, Songs, Books, Actresses, and Characters

The ABW experience plays itself out in record-breaking feats of athleticism, moving poems, best-selling books, chart-topping music, and award-winning films. Without question, our contributions to sports, the literary landscape, music industry, and Hollywood make up some of entertainment's most popular moments. But even more important than what our contributions have given to society is what ABW culture has given to us. Our art is the soundtrack, film, and manuscript that rides out during the good times—like romantic trysts, weddings, and that special time we carve out for our girls—and through the pressure-filled times, like the painful loss of loved ones, or the untimely exit of the one we thought was the One.

Our patron saint for this chapter is Aretha Franklin for recording the classic, chart-topping soul song "Respect." This single was revolutionary for its time, for here was a black woman putting her man on notice—and the country, for that matter—by demanding R-E-S-P-E-C-T! Don't front: Every time you hear this ABW anthem from the Queen of Soul, you just automatically sing along. And it's the message behind this song that fuels many of our most spectacular entertainment moments. Its beat beats in the hearts of actresses as they fight for well-rounded roles, in the hearts of musicians as they put our story into their lyrics, and in those of authors as they chronicle our most intimate moments and thoughts.

To help ABWs celebrate their rich entertainment history, we compiled a list of movies, songs, entertainers, and literature that embody the ABW spirit and demand exactly what Aretha did: Respect! Turn to this list when that coworker incites you to riot, or when your girlfriends come over for a little R&R, after the breakup with that ol' no-good man and just before you embark on a new love journey—or just when you need some good old-fashioned renewal.

ABW MUST-SEE MOVIES, MUST-HEAR ALBUMS, AND MUST-READ LITERATURE

Every now and then, there comes along an album or a movie or a beautiful piece of literature that you just want to curl up with—pieces that bring back memories, make you throw your hands up in exultation, just feel good to your soul. They make us cry, they make us laugh—they make us dance. And they leave us proud to be an ABW. Here's a list of fifty official must-haves for the quintessential ABW.

1. **The flick:** *The Color Purple*
   Why it's a must-see: Girl power rules in this adaptation of the Alice Walker novel of the same name. The all-star cast, including Oprah Winfrey and Whoopi Goldberg, put perfect voice to the ABW's triumph over fear, frustrations, abuse, and adversity at the hands of white folks and no-count men.

2. **The flick:** *How Stella Got Her Groove Back*
   Why it's a must-see: Not only did Angela Bassett prove that age forty is indeed fabulous when she strutted her chiseled body in front of audiences across the land—she and author/producer Terry McMillan, who penned the

novel of the same name, made it officially okay for
women to go for the guy and turn him out.

3. **The flick:** *Mahogany*
Why it's a must-see: What? The Boss—Diana Ross—in
all those beautiful clothes, kissing on Billy Dee Williams
and being a fabulous model living a fabulous life? Who
didn't put on her mama's fake eyelashes, swing her fake
hair, and become a star after this hit the screen?

4. **The flick:** *love jones*
Why it's a must-see: They call it "buppy love," and this
was the first time our generation got to see on-screen
what we all knew from the get: It's easy to fall in love
with the cutie—but, as Isaiah Washington's character so
eloquently put it, how in the hell "do you stay there?"
Thankfully, Nia Long and Larenz Tate helped us figure
it out.

5. **The flick:** *Set It Off*
Why it's a must-see: Frankie (Vivica A. Fox), Cleo
(Queen Latifah), T.T. (Kimberly Elise), and Stony (Jada
Pinkett-Smith) took their friendship to a new level when
they decided to rob banks together to escape the hood.
A true testament to what our girls will do when it comes
time for someone to have your back.

6. **The flick:** *Love & Basketball*
   Why it's a must-see: Never mind that Sanaa Lathan got cut up for the part and learned how to ball like one of the fellas—she showed us it's truly possible to keep the career and get the man, and look good doing it.

7. **The flick:** *Foxy Brown*
   Why it's a must-see: Pam Grier and her Afro kicked some major bell-bottom ass in this flick, showing us that we, too, could be some bad mutha—shut yo' mouths!

8. **The flick:** *Poetic Justice*
   Why it's a must-see: A very grown-up Janet Jackson let thug passion Tupac Shakur show her a thing or two about how to get over heartbreak and learn to love again—whether she liked it or not.

9. **The flick:** *Waiting to Exhale*
   Why it's a must-see: We could all identify somehow with each of the characters—the perpetually in love Robin, the overworked, understimulated Savannah, the overweight single mom Gloria, and the heartbroken Bernadine. But what most stands out is the bond they forged together— and the we-don't-need-a-man-to-be-happy mantra this film adaptation of the Terry McMillan novel espoused.

10. The flick: *A Thin Line between Love and Hate*
Why it's a must-see: With Lynn Whitfield giving Glenn Close a run for her *Fatal Attraction* paycheck, this movie put brothers on notice that we ABWs are neither to be played with nor ignored.

11. The flick: *What's Love Got to Do with It*
Why it's a must-see: Who knew Ike was doing Annie Mae Bullock like that? But when she walks away from his abusive ass with a busted lip but her pride intact, Tina Turner gave all of us inspiration for how to play to win.

12: The flick: *Jungle Fever*
Why it's a must-see: The war council scene, in which Drew Purify's girlfriend's breakdown of why black men ain't shit, is priceless.

13. The flick: *Soul Food*
Why it's a must-see: The Joseph sisters showed us that at the end of the day, your kinfolk is all you've got—well, that and a damn good macaroni and cheese recipe!

14. The flick: *Sparkle*
Why it's a must-see: Ah, the blues of stardom. These sisters showed us that talent means nothing if you don't prepare yourself for success.

15. The flick: *Bamboozled*
    Why it's a must-see: Sure Jada Pinkett-Smith's charac-
    ter, Sloan, slept her way to the top—but her speech about
    how she got her gig because she's smart was inspirational.

16. The book: *Their Eyes Were Watching God* by Zora Neale
    Hurston
    Why it's a must-read: Zora taught us that true love
    isn't about what he's got in his pocket, or even about
    whether he's in his right state of mind—it's about what
    makes a girl's heart flutter. And for sure, we ABWs are
    "da mules of the world," but we don't have to let the
    world ride our asses!

17. The book: *I Know Why the Caged Bird Sings* by Maya
    Angelou
    Why it's a must-read: This piece, based on the true
    story of Maya Angelou's rape and subsequent seven-
    year silence, is true inspiration for all of us who have lost
    our voice—literally and figuratively—and are looking for
    a way to find it again.

18. The book: *The Bluest Eye* by Toni Morrison
    Why it's a must-read: We've all suffered the affliction
    of little Pecola Breedlove, a dark-skinned, kinky-haired
    black girl who wanted to be a white child with the
    blondest hair and the bluest eyes. This piece inspires us

to let go of the ugly girl within and embrace the beauty of our blackness.

19. **The book:** *Disappearing Acts* by Terry McMillan
Why it's a must-read: Another McMillan classic, this novel affirmed for us that if you don't watch yourself, Negroes will take a beautiful black woman for granted— no matter how much they say they're in love. Watch your back, girl.

20. **The book:** *Assata: An Autobiography* by Assata Shakur
Why it's a must-read: Assata kicked ass, took names, and when she got caught, she escaped from a maximum security prison to live life as an exile on Cuba—and to this day, no one knows how the hell she got out. We'd never advocate the killing of cops, but it takes a true ABW to buck the system and The Man—and live to tell about it.

21. **The book:** *For Colored Girls Who Have Considered Suicide When the Rainbow Is Enuf* by Ntozake Shange
Why it's a must-read: It profoundly dramatized the hopes, frustrations, and fears of black women emerging from the civil rights movement and a women's movement that both failed to fully accept them as equal partners.

22. **The book:** *The Sistahs' Rules* by Denene Millner
Why it's a must-read: Not only did our girl Denene

write it, but it's become a cult classic among women seriously looking for true love. Sage advice for how to meet, get, and keep a good one.

23. The book: *Brothers and Sisters* by Bebe Moore Campbell
Why it's a must-read: For any ABW looking for affirmation that it's just not easy to choose loyalties between being a woman and being black, this book, about the choices an African American female banker is forced to make after her black boss sexually harasses her, is required reading.

24. The book: The Bible
Why it's a must-read: It's got the best stories ever about love, betrayal, murder, mayhem, and sex, and even in your deepest, darkest hour, it provides solace the way no one can. God's word: you can't beat it.

25. The play: *Venus* by Suzan-Lori Parks
Why it's a must-see: Based on the true story of Sarah Baartman, the nineteenth-century woman whose butt was so big and fascinating to Europeans that she was put on display as an oddity at a sideshow, Parks's piece showcases the depths we'll go to find love—no matter how much we're being played.

26. **The poem:** "Ego Tripping" by Nikki Giovanni
    Why it's a must-read: Come on, Nikki broke it down so that it will forever be broke when she described just how dope black women are in this classic piece.

27. **The poem:** "Phenomenal Woman" by Maya Angelou
    Why it's a must-read: It's a classic—probably one of the most recited poems by black women everywhere. Why? Because, like "Ego Tripping," it tells the world why we're so fly.

28. **The album:** *The Very Best of Rufus* featuring Chaka Khan
    Why it's a must-have: Although all these little girls who call themselves singers try to emulate her style, Chaka's voice is electric—and unmatched. She's also the master of the come-hither song—"Do You Love What You Feel?," "Dance with Me," and "Sweet Thing" are just as powerful as her "I'm Every Woman" for their ability to seduce. Chaka is, indeed, the sweet thang!

29. **The album:** *Abbey Is Blue* by Abbey Lincoln
    Why it's a must-have: Abbey is so very dope. Not only was she once a groundbreaking actress—she starred opposite Sidney Poitier in *For Love of Ivy*—she was, and still is, also political, deep, beautiful, and a helluva singer. Sit in a candlelit room with a glass of wine, and

slip this album into your CD player. You'll feel like she means every single solitary word—every note—that she sings. It'll make your soul ache.

30. The album: *Private Dancer* by Tina Turner
Why it's a must-have: The comeback album of a lifetime, Tina proves that not even a steel-toe boot can keep a determined ABW down.

31. The album: *Whitney Houston* by Whitney Houston
Why it's a must-have: Before all the madness there was just amazing music—and songs of heartbreak and loving with abandon. This is pure Whitney at her very best!

32. The album: *Rapture* by Anita Baker
Why it's a must-have: With a song for every stage of love under the sun, Anita's silky voice will keep you spellbound from beginning to end.

33. The album: *Control* by Janet Jackson
Why it's a must-have: This masterpiece is filled with the original single black female anthems—all of which celebrate being young, large, and in charge, thank you.

34. The album: *Born to Sing* by En Vogue
Why it's a must-have: These ladies work every range of

the musical bar, and their songs will have you shaking that booty and loving down your man.

35. **The album:** *Love Deluxe* by Sade
Why it's a must-have: Few do it better. This tearjerker actually makes you feel better about the one you lost after you've listened to it.

36. **The album:** *Toni Braxton* by Toni Braxton
Why it's a must-have: Toni's bittersweet tales of love and heartache comfort us when we're down and inspire us to keep it moving, knowing there's other fish in the sea.

37. **The album:** *Plantation Lullabies* by Me'Shell Ndegeocello
Why it's a must-have: In true ABW form, Me'Shell pulls no punches and spares no feelings in this masterpiece that covers race, sexism, and love found and lost like no other artist.

38. **The album:** *My Life* by Mary J. Blige
Why it's a must-have: This ABW icon speaks to us like our tightest girl on this diarylike album. Tissues required.

39. **The album:** *CrazySexyCool* by TLC
Why it's a must-have: When you've got to get up and

go, this trio's music keeps you moving—and on the lookout for that "Red Light Special."

40. The album: *More Than a Melody* by Yolanda Adams
   Why it's a must-have: If there's one thing an ABW knows, it's that she's gotta keep the faith.

41. The album: *Waiting to Exhale Soundtrack* by Various Artists
   Why it's a must-have: The perfect remedy for when you've been holding your breath a little too long.

42. The album: *Faith* by Faith Evans
   Why it's a must-have: No stranger to relationship drama, the widow of the Notorious B.I.G. is the siren behind the beats of our lives. With songs like "Soon As I Get Home," she makes it all right to be a sucker for your man.

43. The album: *Love Jones: The Movie* by Various Artists
   Why it's a must-have: Its laid-back grooves instantly remind you of falling in love—over and over again.

44. The album: *Baduizm* by Erykah Badu
   Why it's a must-have: Each song seems to make the world a better place—one incense stick at a time.

45. **The album:** *The Miseducation of Lauryn Hill* by Lauryn Hill
    Why it's a must-have: Lauryn preaches and teaches about love gained, lost, and played on this album—the soundtrack to a true ABW's life.

46. **The album:** *Black Diamond* by Angie Stone
    Why it's a must-have: Her words of wisdom are delivered in songs that soothe your heart, mind, and soul.

47. **The album:** *Who Is Jill Scott?* by Jill Scott
    Why it's a must-have: Pure neo-soul at its finest, Jill's music offers new ways to be loved down—the right way, for sure.

48. **The album:** *Acoustic Soul* by India.Arie
    Why it's a must-have: Not only is it sonically beautiful, India urges ABWs everywhere to love with abandon and live their best life possible—with no regrets.

49. **The album:** *The Lady Sings* by Billie Holiday
    Why it's a must-have: Billie smolders—her music fills up your soul—and this collection has an anecdote for every last ill-afflicting ABW: "Good Morning Heartache," when he just won't act right; "Body and Soul," when he is; "Ain't Nobody's Business," if you're feeling independent and two-snaps-up carefree; "God Bless

the Child," when your humanitarian side kicks in; and "Strange Fruit," to always remember from whence your people came.

50. **The album:** *Art & Survival* by Dianne Reeves
Why it's a must-have: For any ABW who has ever wanted to stand from the rooftops and tell the world that she is a strong, proud, righteous woman, put this album on for inspiration. With songs that praise the ancestors for strength, beckon us to the river for healing, and tell us to strike out for liberation, one listen and you'll be inspired to move mountains with your bare, freshly manicured hands. "I am an endangered species, but I sing no victim's song," Dianne sings on "Endangered Species." You better recognize!

Of course, there are a host of entertainers—actresses, singers, athletes, directors, and the like—who have represented lovely for us ABWs, crafting the songs, characters, films, and sports moments that make us unbelievably proud to be who we are. Here, our crib sheet of the ABW's top fifty favorite entertainers:

1. **Gloria Gaynor**
Defining moment: "I Will Survive"
This timeless jam always provides inspiration to get you out of the valley.

2. Aretha Franklin
   Defining moment: "R-E-S-P-E-C-T"
   When the Queen of Soul talks, everyone better pay attention. Not to mention, we all deserve it, dammit!

3. Kelis
   Defining moment: "Caught Out There" ("I Hate You So Much Right Now")
   Kelis is the spokeswoman for those times when your relationship has clearly hit a brick wall.

4. Karyn White
   Defining moment: "Superwoman"
   Karyn represented for the ladies by letting men know that there aren't any "S's" emblazoned on our chests and that a cape is not part of our ensemble.

5. Chaka Khan
   Defining moment: "I'm Every Woman"
   This timeless jam will have you walking on air and believing everything is within your grasp.

6. Mary J. Blige
   Defining moment: "Not Gon' Cry"
   MJB makes it crystal clear that there'll be no more time, energy, or Kleenex wasted on a love gone wrong.

7. **Destiny's Child**
   Defining moment: "Independent Woman"
   When you need to celebrate everything that you've accomplished by your damn self, these ladies know how to say it!

8. **TLC**
   Defining moment: "Scrubs"
   This trio put it down for all ABWs by declaring the days of the "good black men shortage" over. We're simply not settling anymore!

9. **Janet Jackson**
   Defining moment: "What Have You Done for Me Lately"
   Miss Jackson had to call a brotha out and we can definitely relate.

10. **Queen Latifah**
    Defining moment: "U.N.I.T.Y."
    Leave it to the Queen to ask the long-overdue question, "Who you callin' a bitch?"

11. **Lauryn Hill**
    Defining moment: "Ex-Factor"
    Instead of playing yourself and asking him for an explanation, let Lauryn do all the begging for you.

12. Tina Turner
Defining moment: "What's Love Got to Do with It?"
Very few are able to put the big picture in perspective like the Queen of Rock and Roll.

13. Erykah Badu
Defining moment: "Tyrone"
Erykah will give you the guts to finally get rid of that tired ass, no-good man.

14. Jill Scott
Defining moment: "He Loves Me (Lyzel in E Flat)"
We're sure that Jill wants every ABW to experience this kind of love.

15. Patti LaBelle
Defining moment: "New Attitude"
Patti helps all of us to realize that every day is a new opportunity to start over.

16. India.Arie
Defining moment: "Video"
When your body image has been badly bruised and needs a little boost, put this tune on and you're guaranteed to feel like a million bucks!

17. Diana Ross
Defining moment: "Coming Out"
The Boss definitely lets the world know that she is on a mission with this disco hit.

18. Donna Summer
Defining moment: "She Works Hard for the Money"
The ultimate disco diva shows her understanding and appreciation for the hell that we go through in our careers.

19. Toni Braxton
Defining moment: "Love Shoulda Brought You Home"
Toni tells it straight up with this jam about an unfaithful scrub.

20. Klymaxx
Defining moment: "Meeting in the Ladies Room"
This classic is perfect for gearing up to spend time with your girls.

21. Mahalia Jackson
Defining moment: "Precious Lord"
The original gospel songbird lets us know that there is always a higher being present when we're feeling all alone.

22. Roxanne Shante
Defining moment: "Roxanne's Revenge"
Sometimes you gotta take it back to the old school with these Negroes.

23. Mariah Carey
Defining moment: "Someday"
Provides perfect theme music for preparing for that annoying class reunion as well as making a trifling ex-boyfriend rue the day he broke your heart.

24. Halle Berry
Defining moment: *The Dorothy Dandridge Movie,* Dorothy Dandridge
It may have taken an Oscar for America to notice Halle, but we've loved her since she brought this ABW icon to life for all the world to celebrate.

25. Angela Bassett
Defining moment: *Waiting to Exhale,* Bernadine "Bernie" Harris
When she tossed her cigarette into that lame-behind Uncle Tom's BMW, Angela took a stand for every single ABW who has ever felt insecure about her nappy roots beside Pollyanna's blonde locks.

26. Esther Rolle
Defining moment: *Good Times* (TV series), Florida Evans

As the face of down-and-out, living-in-the-project, economically challenged ABWs everywhere, she epitomized the mythical strong black woman who is able to carry an entire family on her back without ever breaking down.

27. Sanaa Lathan
Defining moment: *Love & Basketball*, Monica Wright

Not only did she hold her own on the basketball court, but this stunner also stood her ground on the playing field of love and in the end was the true champion.

28. Gabrielle Union
Defining moment: *Bring It On*, Conny Spalding

Who can ever forget the classic "don't try me" ABW attitude that Gabrielle exemplified as she worked it out and led her squad to a cheerleading championship?

29. Debbie Allen
Defining moment: *Fame* (TV series), Lydia Grant

When she broke down the cost of becoming a star, it was like she was lighting the fire under all of our asses.

30. Ruby Dee
Defining moment: *Jungle Fever*, Lucinda Purify

She set fire to the Broadway stage and big-screen versions of *A Raisin in the Sun*, but it was this performance that tore your heart in two as she tried to save her eldest from a life of drugs.

31. Whoopi Goldberg
Defining moment: *The Color Purple*, Celie
When she put that two-fingered hex on Mister, everyone became an instant believer in the power of "roots."

32. Oprah
Defining moment: *The Oprah Winfrey Show* (TV series)
She took a local talk show and turned it into an international multibillion-dollar corporation with a cultlike following. She is officially the ruler of the world!

33. Queen Latifah
Defining moment: *Set It Off*, Cleopatra "Cleo" Sims
The Queen held it down harder than a whole lot of men we know!

34. Vivica A. Fox
Defining moment: *Soul Food*, Maxine
She effortlessly brought the image of the hardworking, down-for-her-family, make-it-happen ABW to life.

35. Mo'Nique
Defining moment: *The Parkers* (TV series), Nikki Parker

Mo'Nique always represents for the big, strong, sexy ABWs who are so much more than "a pretty face."

36. Vanessa Williams
Defining moment: 1984 Miss America Pageant, winner
Despite the porn pictures and the unfortunate dethroning incident, she still managed to become a celebrated singer, award-winning actress, wife of an NBA superstar, and to have a beautiful family—proving beyond a doubt that you can make mistakes and still have it all!

37. Nia Long
Defining moment: *Boyz N the Hood*, Brandi
With her amazing looks and sweet personality, she completely embodied the fly girl next door who we all secretly desired to be down with.

38. Jada Pinkett-Smith
Defining moment: *A Different World* (TV series), Lena James
With her sassy mouth and take-no-shorts attitude, it was immediately clear that the future Mrs. Will Smith was destined to run the show.

39. Diahann Carroll
Defining moment: *The Diahann Carroll Show*, herself
As the very first African American woman to headline a

TV show, it was only natural for her to star as Dominque, then the only independently wealthy black female socialite on the classic prime-time series *Dynasty*.

40. Dorothy Dandridge
Defining moment: *Carmen Jones,* Carmen Jones
As one of the the first universally accepted black sex symbols, Dorothy set beauty standards ABWs are still aspiring to this very day.

41. Lynn Whitfield
Defining moment: *A Thin Line between Love and Hate,* Brandi Web
Despite naysayers' criticisms of her being the wrong person for the role, Lynn came back and killed it. Her larger-than-life ABW blackout was breathtaking. She put Glenn Close to shame.

42. Lena Horne
Defining moment: *Cabin in the Sky,* Georgia Brown
She was the first black woman to wield enough beauty and star power in Hollywood to refuse the stereotypical mammy roles reserved for women of color.

43. Gina Prince-Bythewood
Defining moment: *Love & Basketball,* producer/director
Straight out of the box, she kicked ass and took names

with her first flick—one that was beautifully filmed, brilliantly directed, and forever cemented in the ABW lexicon of the greatest films of all time. We watch this one at least once a month.

44. Kasi Lemmons
Defining moment: *Eve's Bayou*, producer/director
In her directorial debut, she managed to chronicle a sitting-on-the-edge-of-our-seat mystery of a clique of Louisiana belles that was smart, graceful, and stylish. Made us darn proud.

45. Marion Jones
Defining moment: 2002 Olympic Games, Australia
Marion won three gold medals, two bronze medals in sprint events, and proved beyond a doubt that she is the fastest woman alive.

46. Venus Williams
Defining moment: 1998 U.S. Open, United States
Changing the face of women's tennis forever, Venus proved that not only do black people play tennis, but we also excel and surpass every imaginable limit.

47. Serena Williams
Defining moment: 1999 Grand Slam Cup, Germany
The world already knew that the Williams sisters were

no joke, but when baby sis put the pounding on Venus, we witnessed the beginning of what has become an extensive domination of the former "whites only" sport.

48. Laila Ali
Defining moment: October 2000 Super Middleweight Championship Bout
By unanimous decision, Muhammad Ali's daughter proved that the apple never falls too far from the tree.

49. Althea Gibson
Defining moment: 1956 Roland Garros, France
In addition to being the first black player to compete in the U.S. grass tournaments, she was the first African American woman to win a major tournament title by beating out the favored British sweetheart, Angela Mortimer.

50. Sheryl Swoopes
Defining moment: Nike Women's Air Swoopes
In addition to being one of the pioneers of women's professional basketball, she was the first woman to have a Nike basketball shoe named after her.

12

iF ABWS RuLeD THe WORLD

Robin Williams said it best on his 2002 HBO special when he suggested the war on Afghanistan and the hunt for Osama bin Laden would have been cut short had the United States sent a few ABWs overseas. For sure, Robin was on to something—but his joke's not all that original. Comedians across the land have made us the butt of their comedy routines by talking about our attitudes and quick-to-cut-ya wit—and suggesting that our nastiness makes everyone just fall in line. To some extent, we agree, though we prefer to credit it not to attitude, but to our herculean ability to get things done. Need your kid to get right? We can do it. Need your man to stop cutting up? We can do it. Boss getting on your nerves? White folks testing you a little too much? Feel like there are some issues that others need to address when it comes to giving us black women respect? We got it covered.

Why? Because we're just a little bit more willing than most others to push decorum out the window in favor of getting the job done. If that means your feelings will get hurt—so be it. ABWs know that the end more than justifies the means, and after it's all said and done, we all win.

Our patron saint? The almighty Oprah. She came from humble beginnings, was bullied by many, and is now one of the most powerful women in the world. She persevered through her issues with weight, appearance, and social acceptance and now lords over a billion-dollar enterprise. She uses her popular TV show to shed light on important topics and effect change in a way that no other woman in history ever has: She's bringing women together and empowering us to live our best lives ever! Dammit—Oprah for president!

Here, a glimpse at what a wonderful world this would be if ABWs were large and in charge.

If ABWs ruled the world . . .

1. Somebody would be making designer clothes that actually fit our waists and our hips—and that annoying pucker in every last pair of our pants and skirts would be banished from existence.

2. Mike Tyson would be the sideshow attraction at a traveling carnival—in Russia.

3. R. Kelly would be missing several body parts.

4. We'd get equal pay for equal work—and an extra 30 percent in our checks every time some man heaped his job responsibilities on us and pretended he was simply "delegating." (Of course, we'd be so well paid, eventually we wouldn't have to work.)

5. The workday would end at 3:00 P.M., giving us just enough time to get our doobies tightened up at the salon, then get home to tell our maid and personal chef what to cook and serve us for dinner.

6. The medical research community would figure out why specific diseases like fibroids, diabetes, stroke, and others *really* affect black women—instead of pretending that our well-being isn't important enough to bother studying.

7. Any rapper who called a black woman a bitch/ho/chickenhead/gold digger/trick or exploited her body parts to make his video look "hot" would be cursed with poor record sales and an inability to, uh, "perform"—

both onstage and off—and forced to trade in his Escalade for a minivan with a Baby on Board sticker in the window and his Rocawear for Top-Siders and corduroys.

8. Any guy who said he would call and then didn't would be cursed with the inability to put together a coherent sentence anytime he tried to talk to "holla" at someone of the opposite sex.

9. There would be no need for an overpriced defense budget—with a country full of angry black women, the rest of the world would just be scared.

10. Every black female actress over age thirty would have the bomb leading role in a blockbuster movie on the big screen—and Morris Chestnut would be the leading man *every time*.

11. There would have been no hanging chads and George Bush would be on a ranch in Texas somewhere, raising cattle and trying his best not to choke on pretzels.

12. Our husbands would have our dinner waiting on the stove—hot—when we came home from work, they'd willingly give the kids their baths and tuck them into

bed, then give us massages before bedtime—and the words "you 'sleep?" would never be uttered—ever—when our eyes are closed and our bodies are in a prone position on the bed.

13. The chick at the fast-food counter/department store register/tollbooth would understand that just because she hates her job doesn't mean she has to be an ass to us, and she'd get a new gig that would make her much more happy.

14. The predominately white audiences who dare to boo and otherwise disrespect Venus and Serena Williams as they step onto the court would have to wait until the year 2022 for the next white Wimbledon champion.

15. There would be no education crisis in our school systems because we would spend as much per student as they do in the best private school system. Where would we get the cash? From the defense budget. (See #9.)

16. Schools would have fewer discipline problems because there would be an effective mix of women and men in teaching positions, making a *real* living wage and happy to come to work in the morning.

17. Every child miscreant would wake up tomorrow and be good—out of fear that his mom will invite an ABW into the home to straighten his little tail out.

18. Every white person who thinks he's cool because he can say a few slang words and owns a Snoop Dogg CD would be cursed to hear only old Barry Manilow showtunes whenever a song plays.

19. Manolo Blahniks and Jimmy Choo shoes would cost $49.99 a pair—and our size would *always* be available.

20. Lauryn Hill would climb out of whatever self-imposed exile she put herself into and teach the world through her music and Lil' Kim would put on some clothes and get to know Jesus.

21. Me'Shell Ndegeocello would be a superstar.

22. White women would understand that our struggle—economic, racial, sex—is their struggle—and that our working together would help us all to defeat the real enemy: men.

23. Any man who dared catcall with the tired, "Yo chocolate, do fries come with that milkshake?"—and other

nonwitty approach lines—would be sentenced to a year's worth of daily recitals of Maya Angelou's poem "Phenomenal Woman"—in front of his boys.

24. Oprah would run for president and be all right with the pay cut and lessening of power.

25. Eleanor Holmes Norton would be in charge of revamping the increasingly Republican Supreme Court lineup—and the first to go would be Clarence "Uncle Tom" Thomas, who would be replaced by, yes, Anita Hill.

26. There would be a national ABW Day (no, this would not be April 1).

27. Everyone would recognize this simple concept: When Mama's not happy, nobody's happy.

28. Food specialists would find a way to make fried chicken, macaroni and cheese, and cornbread nonfattening, tasty, *and* good for you.

29. All the major channels would play home, gardening, and decorating shows on Sundays, and men would have to find something to do with the kids while we sipped wine and hogged the remote.

30. It would be a crime for hairdressers to overbook clients, and sticking to appointments would be law.

31. The WNBA season would go from November to June, and the NBA would be broadcast for the scant six weeks in the summertime, so the cute boys can run around in their little shorts. On second thought, scratch that: We'll take as many months of the latter as we can possibly get.

32. The women of the WNBA would each have their own personal hairstylist who would be commissioned to travel with them on *every* road trip—they should, after all, look dope on the road.

33. We could look forward to a Roy Jones fight every weekend—he does, after all, have to take care of all them kids and chickens.

34. Life of the average college campus would revolve around the women's soccer and basketball teams and they could get away with rape, murder, and near illiteracy. On second thought, let's leave that to the boys.

35. Instead of worshiping the latest $200 sneaker with some untouchable celebrity baller's name on the side, our kids would anxiously search the bookstores for authors like

Ezra Jack Keats, Nikki Giovanni, James Baldwin, and Zora Neale Hurston.

36. Black children everywhere would be able to recite their multiplication tables and black history as handily as they do the latest Jay-Z song.

37. Men would just, like, get it.

38. Our clothes would be dry-cleaned for a reasonable price, and men would have to pay $5.99 each to get their cotton shirts washed and pressed—even when they're the same exact material as the shirts we get dry-cleaned for $.99.

39. No child would ever be hungry.

40. There'd be no such thing as rape, assault, and domestic violence—it'd be one strike against a woman and you're out.

41. Birth control would be covered by insurance—just like Viagra.

42. There'd be birth control for men.

43. All companies would be required to provide paid maternity leave for both parents for a year.

44. The height and weight chart would be less ideal, much more realistic.

45. There would be no need for affirmative action—everything would simply be equal.

46. You could claim your hairdresser as a dependent on your taxes.

47. All men would be required to register their dating status in a national registry so that we could all be clear on who's dating and who's really single.

48. Men would receive tax deductions for taking state-funded classes on how to please their women in bed.

49. There would be no taxes on household necessities like jewels, shoes, and handbags.

50. The world would just be a better place.

13

100 Things That Make ABWs Happy

After reading this book, some may jump to the incorrect conclusion that ABWs are too hard to please and never happy or satisfied. Many think that we're always gritting our teeth, swiveling our necks, and cursing somebody out. Sure, between incompetent coworkers, out-of-control kids, and racists, things might seem challenging for us at times. But even the angriest ABW knows that you can't be angry all the time.

So what makes us happy? This question has multiple answers so we thought we'd just compile a superlong list of things, situations, and people that make us smile, giggle, cry tears of joy, and give us stomach cramps from laughing so hard. As you will see, it's really just the simple things—okay, and one big sparkly thing—that make us rejoice. You may want to copy this chapter for your friends and errant family members and post on your cubicle at work so folks will know how to get on your good side.

1. Pedicures: Nothing says happy like a set of pretty feet. Plus, if you have to put your foot in someone's behind later in the day, at least it will look good.

2. New fragrance

3. Reunions: Even when the cousins start fighting over bid whiz, it's all good.

4. An empty in-box: It usually doesn't last long, but it's nice to have all your work completed. Hide it for a couple of days so they can't give you any more work.

5. Sunday morning

6. A new album by Mary J. Blige: Each track sounds like she can see everything that's going on in our lives and never fails to deliver musical therapy for all types of situations.

7. Hugs from our kids: There's nothing like their little arms wrapped around our necks to bring out a smile. And the smile lasts a long time if they aren't doing it to get out of something.

8. A kiss on the neck from our man: This also has the power to diffuse most tense situations instantly.

9. The new E. Lynn Harris novel: Catching up with our favorite characters makes us howl with laughter so we're the first ones in the store to pick up his latest page-turner.

10. Making the last credit card payment: Admittedly, we're going to run the "only for emergencies card" right back up again next month, but we still smile when we write that last check.

11. Resigning from a bad job: Last day on the job is the perfect time to let everyone know just how much you've "enjoyed" working with them.

12. A fresh touch-up

13. A new dress

14. Graduations

15. When our *Essence* magazine subscription arrives: We get spiritual renewal, head-to-toe beauty, and fashion advice as we flip through the pages of our favorite magazine each month.

16. Catching *The Cosby Show* reruns: must-see TV for lots of laughs

17. Sweet potato pie: good to the last forkful

18. Thanksgiving: With all our loved ones around, it's nothing but good times—until Uncle June Bug gets drunk again, of course.

19. Ghetto weddings: From the bridal party's choreographed moves as they enter the church to the Electric Slide jam at the reception, these events are always good for lots of laughs and sweating out your relaxer.

20. Concert tickets

21. Our mamas: From our real mothers to our play mothers, they always know just what to say to get us to smile.

22. Girls' night: It's nothing but laughs when you get together with your girls.

23. Venus and Serena Williams: Watching these two tennis phenoms wipe the court with the competition makes us smile with pride.

24. White folks caught on the news: We're smiling just because we're glad it isn't somebody we know heading to jail.

25. Brunch

26. Finding a stamp in the bottom of your bag

27. A good joke: Whether it comes from a concert special or one of the beauticians at the beauty shop, a gut-buster is always welcome.

28. Getting a seat on a crowded bus or subway car: On the right day, this can feel like winning the lottery.

29. When somebody pays us back after borrowing money

30. Hearing "that song" on the radio: Memories come flooding back and suddenly we're swaying back and forth, eyes closed, using our hairbrush as a microphone.

31. Getting a mortgage: Weezie and George ain't got nothing on us today.

32. Sweet tea: always hits the spot

33. Room service: Anytime we don't have to buy the groceries, prepare the meal, and serve it, we'll smile.

34. Freshly laundered sheets: guarantees a good night's sleep

35. New red shoes

36. A new hat

37. When you can buy something special for your parents

38. Getting saved

39. BBQ ribs: finger-lickin' good

40. The new Morris Chestnut movie: Half the time we don't even know what the plot of the movie is, but as soon as this fine man hits the screen, we're riveted.

41. News that your girlfriend is pregnant

42. Baby showers: What's more fun than opening boxes full of teeny-tiny clothes?

43. Fitting into something that once was relegated to the "size I used to wear" section of the closet: It may not fit next week, but we'll be smiling our big ass off in it today.

44. Voting

45. The first time your new puppy goes to the bathroom outside

46. Kicking off our shoes after a long, hard day

47. Foot massage

48. New hair color: It's like getting a new lease on your love life.

49. Receiving pictures in the mail

50. The "let's get back together" call

51. Just-got-back-together sex

52. Watching *The Color Purple:* We run the range of emotions in this movie as we recite every line.

53. A chilled mimosa

54. Our favorite passage in the Bible: Sometimes you have to read it a few times depending on the reason you're calling on the Word.

55. A shoe sale: Sometimes we might even yell hallelujah if we luck up on an additional discount at the register.

56. New underwear

57. Finding ten dollars in the pocket of a pair of pants we'd forgotten about

58. Getting promoted: We're smiling until we realize our new title comes with the same salary and more work.

59. Getting our scalp scratched and oiled: If administered properly, we may even fall asleep with a smile on our face.

60. Our dads: when they tell us they are proud of us

61. A new handbag

62. Your kid's artwork

63. Anything chocolate at the end of a hard day: A good piece of chocolate cake, cookie, or candy offers guilt-free therapy.

64. An unexpected flower delivery: It's a full-on grin if he sent them "just because."

65. Slow dancing: If it's with the right guy, it makes us feel like we're a teenager again, back at a basement party.

66. When our children perform

67. The smell of a fresh spring morning

68. Making it to the end of the month with money in the bank

69. Our tax-return check

70. School pictures

71. Baby smells, except for one smell, of course

72. The first time our babies say "Mama": It takes them forever and for some reason "Dada" always comes first.

73. A good sermon

74. When a complete stranger compliments us: not a crazy or smelly stranger or somebody trying to get our number

75. Oprah

76. New lipstick

77. A new Mercedes-Benz

78. When a black man opens or holds the door for us

79. When you glance at the church bulletin and see that your favorite choir is singing today

80. A freshly painted room in your new apartment

81. When "our song" comes on in the club

82. A phone call from a long-lost friend: Of course she gets cursed out for being MIA for so long, and then you talk for hours.

83. Watching our children sleep: When the little devils are asleep they look like angels sent from heaven.

84. Receiving a voice mail from the guy you just met

85. A good report card

86. The first time

87. Calling in sick when there's nothing wrong

88. The big "O": followed by your man getting you a cold beverage

89. Easter Sunday

90. When our hair finally grows out from a bad cut: We haven't smiled in months, so this time it's a big one.

91. Planting flowers in our garden

92. Good gossip

93. Finding a good pair of jeans

94. The marriage proposal

95. Holidays that fall on a Monday

96. A surprise birthday party

97. When people enjoy our cooking

98. When we receive a financial windfall: It's rare, but when it happens, look out!

99. Getting the last laugh

100. Dear Reader: You fill in this last one _____